Tomorrow's Community College

Roy W. Smith

Life Press, Inc.

Library of Congress Catalog Number 95-79403

Smith, Roy W.

Tomorrow's Community College

Published by

Life Press, Inc.

Printed by

Princeton Academic Press

I.S.B.N. 0-9648119-8-7

Printed in the United States of America

This Essay is Dedicated

to My Sister

Virginia L. Busch

Contents

Preface

Over the past century, the community college movement in America has grown dramatically, and has gained respect and stature. But it has not gained the respect or the stature nationally that many community college leaders believe it deserves. It is serving an ever increasing proportion of those enrolled in institutions of higher education in America. And it is serving an ever increasing number of older adults, minority students and disadvantaged students who enroll because community colleges are accessible, affordable, service-oriented, and student-friendly.

Although community colleges serve some 11 million students nationally and are often called the people's institutions of higher education, they are not well understood by the general public nor by public officials or other policymakers. Even those people involved directly with community colleges, including governing board members, often do not fully appreciate the potential of these innovative institutions.

To a limited degree, political leaders and other policymakers have recently begun to look to the community college to help solve major national, regional and state issues, because community colleges have proven they can produce — and produce inexpensively. Many of these political leaders and other policymakers throughout the nation are familiar with the basic outlines of the community college philosophy, but they do not seem to have an in-depth understanding of what the movement is about and what it can do — and, just as importantly, cannot and should not do. The community college idea seems great, but the depth and the importance of what community colleges accomplish is understood to only a limited degree.

Political leaders and other policymakers and the general public need to be alerted to the vast, untapped potential of the community college. With greater knowledge about the community college concept, federal, state and local policymakers would take greater advantage of these flexible, accessible and cost-effective institutions. They should look to the community college to help solve major national and regional issues such as illiteracy, drug abuse, workforce development and welfare reform and many others. With adequate funding — a small amount in the bigger picture of trillion-dollar budgets — they could provide a national network that could have a vast impact on a society hungry for both information and understanding.

Public officials, other policymakers and the general public also need to have some idea of the future directions of the community college mission — a mission that will be greatly influenced by trends and developments that can already be foreseen. These trends and developments resulting from a changing America within a changing world will eventually force every community college to look to the future and to plan strategically — to take an extensive look at their competitors for students, for dollars, for faculty and staff and for programs. While meeting the specific needs of the constituents they service, community colleges at the same time can help to remedy some of the national issues badly in need of resolution.

Having been part of the community college movement for more than 35 years, I have seen community colleges grow and develop into a major component of this nation's system of higher education. I have been fortunate to view this growth and development from both an independent and a public perspective. I have also been fortunate to view the community college movement from the perspective of an administrator as well as secretary of the governing boards for more than 25 years, providing a governance perspective as well.

A journalist by profession, I joined Union Junior College in Cranford, N. J. in 1957 as director of public relations to assist in its Silver Anniversary Development Fund campaign, and in 1967 I was appointed the College's first vice president. Over the years the vice president title changed from time to time but it always involved external and public affairs and some other assignments. Officially and unofficially I have had the great experience over the years of sampling nearly every position and every activity available at the College with the vital exception of teaching. And in 1989 and 1990 I served as acting president for 16 months — an exhilarating experience with great challenges, some successes and a feeling of real accomplishment.

I have been most fortunate to have had mentors of exceptional scope and depth in their understanding of higher education and its impact on society. In particular, Dr. Kenneth C. MacKay, who was president of Union College for more than 25 years and is often called the father of the community college in New Jersey. He is a man of wry wit, great scholarship and vast insight into the community college philosophy. Another is Dr. Albert E. Meder, Jr., dean of the university-emeritus, Rutgers—The State University of New Jersey, New Brunswick, N. J., who was the "man behind the scene" who kept Rutgers moving ahead dynamically as presidents came and went and who was a major force on the Commission on Higher Education of the Middle States Association of Colleges and Schools, the regional accrediting agency, for many years. Dr. Meder served as chair of the Educational Policy Committee of the Board of Trustees of Union Junior College and Union College for more than 25 years. No one with whom I am familiar understands the role of higher education and how higher education operates better or more comprehensively than Dr. Meder.

Furthermore, Union County College has had a most unique history, which also provided an opportunity for me to develop varied and broad perspectives about the community college movement. It was founded in 1933 under the title of Union County Junior College as an Emergency Relief Administration project of the Great

Depression designed primarily to provide employment for out-of-work professors and secondarily to provide higher education for men and women who could not afford to go to college. As always happens, federal funds ran out in 1936 and the College was organized as an independent institution under the title of Union Junior College — a role it maintained through 1968. (In 1966, it changed its name to Union College.) It became a quasi-public institution in 1969, providing community college services in lieu of a County College (as community colleges are known in New Jersey). And in 1982 it merged with a public technical institute under the title of Union County College as Union County's public community college. (How this was accomplished is spelled out in two volumes, "New Jersey's Union College" by Dr. Donald Raichle and "The Remaking of A College" by Roy W. Smith.)

So after 100 years of service, the American community college system has developed a sense of complacency — a sense that the status quo or business as usual is good enough. Some of this smugness can be attributed to college leaders who feel more comfortable riding the wave of today's successes, failing to appreciate that America and the world are changing dramatically. This is unfortunate, since the community college movement up to now has been dynamic and progressive.

The American community college movement is at a crossroads: a time to consolidate, stabilize and maintain the status quo or a time to move forward with a broader, richer, more diverse mission. In view of the current political climate and of the limited resources available, it would be easier and safer for most community colleges to maintain the status quo. But political, economic and social forces — a changing America within a changing world — will project most community colleges into a broader, richer, more diverse mission, and into leadership roles to help in a significant way to solve some of America's major problems.

This essay, therefore, is designed to provoke discussion about where the community college movement in America should go in the future. This discussion needs to include trustees, chief executive officers, faculty, staff, alumni and students. And it needs to include local, state and national leaders — policymakers at all levels — as well as the general public. Perhaps this essay can provide some background and some ideas to generate debate that will lead to a broader, more comprehensive community college system in America.

Foreword

Community college board members, who read Roy W. Smith's essay — as we urge them to do — before the next board meeting are likely upon completion of their reading either to resign their board seats or, it may be hoped, become infused with enough of Smith's conviction and enthusiasm to resolve to give full attention to the position. His long, successful career as a junior college official, his extraordinary experience from inside, and most of all, his vision of the community college in its myriad catalog of opportunities in that brave new world beyond Year 2000, all this he distills into a quite dazzling concept of his college being the logical vehicle for change in a changing America and world.

For those of us, the less hardy type, battered by the slings and disenchantments of time, or too indolent or arthritic, questions naturally arise. So splendid a panorama must have its imperfections. Even as Woodrow Wilson's League of Nations, so Roy Smith's Community College appears too good to be true. Nevertheless, it is recommended reading for those in whose hands will be the education of tomorrow. Its opportunities become a formidable challenge.

The caveats are not about Smith's vision of tomorrow. They much more implicate imperfections of the present, some of which are residual to the junior college movement. A suggestion: Smith now should address himself to those problems of today which well may impede the role of the college in his future America.

It would be helpful if Smith now apply his experience in both college and community (in its broad sense) to comment on alleged, apparent or very real shortcomings of this very

American community institution, frailties which have come to light in its now not really brief existence. After all, as Smith points out, this type of college is no longer a fledgling. It approaches a century of trial and error.

Specifically, the community colleges' emphasis on its oft-repeated "open door," its need for deep-pocket tax support, its proliferation of programs, its wary, often covert competition with more venerable institutions (even if brightly packaged in mutual service aphorisms), its extensive utilization of adjunct faculty, these and other vexing issues loom large enough to deserve thoughtful analysis by someone who has seen it quite all, inside and out, warts and all.

For example, or in fact for two examples, how can we cope with such emerging aspects of the community college as its swift-growing function in providing remedial or developmental studies — for high school underachievers? There is extant a feeling that something is wrong with a system which requires widespread repetition of high school work. Smith's essay does emphasize that the community college has to be higher education. Wherever the fault lies — in the grades or elsewhere — the problem needs study. To recognize it in no way derogates the splendid efforts of so many deserving students taking advantage of the second chance, truly inspirational in many instances.

The second example concerns, as Smith states, the necessity for institutional leadership of the highest order, in short, a President fit to lead. As the community college loses the radiant glow of youth, increasingly higher expectations call for administrative competence and the ability for intellectual leadership. Often these questions are asked by those rightfully suspicious of political pressures exerted locally and — it has been known to happen — through boards of trustees. Often it happens college boards shed a portion of their responsibility and governance to embrace now the all-inclusive "search committee" in the selection of a president. This glamorously new device, with all the novel freshness of the Grateful Dead, offers all the comforts of political correctness (being democratic, for example, means having at least one undergraduate on the committee). Expense-paid junkets to faraway places to interview candidates are much more appealing to committee members than, say, to taxpayers. Selecting a president should be as serious a business as engaging a basketball coach or a winning season on the court, gridiron or wrestling mats.

Of course, more familiar issues can be raised of the community colleges in the brave new world. Is the college spreading itself too thin? Does it disregard the moral instructions of the church-related institutions?

Do not many of the problems of the future have to be solved outside the college? For sure, Smith is correct in stating that in its mission, the community college must be intimately involved with all the other parts of the community whole. No one part can do the job alone.

In conclusion, we clear the way for Smith's next essay, his *arrière-pensée*, his afterthoughts on the now and heretofore. We have already enjoyed his journey to the edges of tomorrow.

Dr. Kenneth C. MacKay
Fairfax, VT.

President Emeritus
Union College
Cranford, N. J.

Past Director
American Association
of Community Colleges

Part I

By Way of Introduction

Today's community college is a vital part of America's extensive system of higher education. The community college is no longer the forgotten or unnoticed stepchild or the second cousin of that system. It has emerged as an equal partner with the four-year colleges and universities. About 12 million Americans are enrolled as undergraduates in all institutions of higher education (about five percent of the entire population) and 43 percent of them attend a community college. Forty percent of all institutions of higher education in America are community colleges.

As in all societies, ours is changing. Now, however, the changes are faster and more profound caused by an explosion of knowledge and rapid, world-wide communications systems like the Internet that reach virtually every corner of the world. For the first time in history, we can see a war in real time on our TV screen, as in Iraq and Bosnia, or view the death of a nation, as in Somalia or Sudan. But this is only the beginning. Now we have more information than we can absorb, analyze and digest. We are increasingly subjected to more and more propaganda. This means that to a degree never envisioned in the past, a well-educated society is needed to comprehend these changes, to understand the implications of change, to analyze them critically and to develop rational answers and rational directions. An inadequately educated society is a critical problem. It is the community college in the future that must play a major role in developing a more highly educated society for America.

As community colleges continue to grow and prosper, they will be asked by society — and by some enlightened political leaders — to do more; to help solve more problems of society, and to make up for the deficiencies of other agencies — particularly the failures of our school system. It may be that America will be creating a "new" community college that is broader in mission, more comprehensive in programming and more open to more people and to more segments of the society. In particular, they will serve the disadvantaged, minorities, urban and rural residents, and senior citizens who will live longer with greater need of intellectual stimulation.

Tomorrow's community college will be an ever more important part of America's system of higher education, because of these significant changes emerging across America that place the community college at the center of the nation's public policy decision-making. Therefore, the future is very promising for the community college movement, as increasingly public officials, opinion leaders and other policymakers are discovering them — discovering how many services they provide, how well they can provide them, and how many national and regional problems they can help solve.

For example, Labor Secretary Robert Reich speaks often about the role of the community college in workforce development, and President Bill Clinton recognized the community colleges speaking at the 75th annual convention of the American Association of Community Colleges in 1995 when he said, "This whole community college movement has made as big a contribution to the future of America as any institutional change in the United States in decades."

"Why do community colleges work?" President Clinton asked. "Well first of all, they're not encumbered by old-fashioned bureaucracies. By and large, they are highly entrepreneurial. They are highly flexible. They are really democratic — small 'd' — they're open to everybody. And people work together. And when something doesn't work they go do something else."

As important issues of the times are discussed, such as welfare reform, job training and economic development, it is the community college that is cited as a major mechanism to help solve them. And policymakers are on the right track. It is the community college that has the flexibility, the experience and the willingness to tackle these and other issues of the times. Furthermore, this is the least expensive way to provide undergraduate education, and data show clearly that the community college does it as effectively as its four-year counterpart. Many policymakers now realize that more students should be directed to community colleges simply to save public funds — if for no other reason. For another thing, the American economy is changing, forcing many people in the workforce to retrain for new jobs — some workers are being forced to retrain a number of times simply to remain employed. It is the community college that can provide many of these services.

Middle class America is now discovering the community college. Parents now are more comfortable sending their children to the hometown community college and then helping them continue their studies at the four-year college or university — even through graduate work. The stigma of attending an open admissions institution is losing its sting, making it more comfortable for high school graduates to select a community college as their first choice. (Americans would be amazed to learn how many of the four-year institutions are nearly "open admissions" colleges by practice if not by policy. The really selective are few.)

Americans also are discovering that community colleges can serve young people who are not ready to go to college away from home. By staying home for a year or two, they become more mature and better prepared to handle the rigors of the large universities or the far-from-home campuses that are not always student-friendly. Community colleges continue to provide a second and even a third opportunity for those who do not make it in the four-year

3

college or university — the only role that many people seem to attribute to the community college.

More parents now attend the local community college themselves to upgrade their skills or to prepare for new professions. Many community colleges now attract those with Ph.D.s and other advanced degrees, who update their computer skills or learn a foreign language or seek intellectual stimulation in some discipline.

Women attending college for the first time have discovered the community college as an attractive way for them to break into higher education. Low-cost, broad-based programming and extensive student support services have been attractive to them, but mostly they found campuses that welcomed them with open arms — as well as open admissions. Today more women than men attend community colleges and the gap is getting larger. Today women represent 58 percent of all community college students.

Many young people as well as their parents and other adults have discovered that community college faculty teach rather than publish or do research. They have discovered that the community college emphasizes teaching and learning and that most faculty members are dedicated to teaching, mentoring and advising.

More and more Americans are looking to their local community college for all kinds of community services, ranging from basic literacy instruction to cultural arts presentations. These community services often include programs for school children — many designed to complement the efforts of the local school systems — and for senior citizens, a growing constituency with extensive needs that higher education can provide.

For many Americans, however, the local community college is still an institution down the road or around the corner where kids from other families go, where their neighbors attend, or where a colleague down the corridor enrolls. For many Americans, the local community college is still seen as a second- or third-choice institution for their children to attend. But these attitudes are changing, as community colleges become better known, serve broader constituencies, and offer a wider range of programs and services.

The size and scope and the comprehensive missions of these two-year institutions are not fully understood by many — probably most — Americans. Over the years, community colleges have not adequately explained their missions and roles and have not adequately promoted themselves and what they do. The task is not easy, because the perception of the media and of the public is that four is better than two no matter the circumstances. Community colleges could enhance their image greatly by working together more closely to sell the good idea that community colleges represent. Some efforts are made through national and state organizations, but mostly each institution tends to sell itself without explaining well the basic philosophy of the community college movement. Undoubtedly, there are many outstanding four-year colleges and universities and many outstanding two-year colleges in America. The press and the public are aware of the prestigious four-year institutions, but few can recognize or even list several of the outstanding two-year colleges. One of the problems, of course, is that the community college is community-oriented, serving a limited constituency and a single region. They hardly ever achieve national attention and there are few positive reasons why they should. They only gain national attention for negative reasons such as a crime or scandal of some kind on campus. Even an outstanding, nationally ranked community college football team cannot gain the headlines such as Notre Dame, Miami, UCLA, or Nebraska, for example, or even Weber State.

In this transitional period of a changing America within a changing world, the nation in its two-century history has never needed community colleges more. America badly requires the kinds of services community colleges provide. It is logical and appropriate, therefore, for the nation to use the vast, existing resource called the community college more extensively and more comprehensively.

Part II

A Changing America
Within A Changing World

The world is in disarray — unsettled and dangerous. The Cold War is over, but the form of the post-Cold War world has yet to emerge.

Clearly, the world is in a period of transition. As Vaclav Havel, president of the Czech Republic, said, "something else is painfully being born." Havel was speaking about the end of the modern age, but it applies today to world affairs, too. "It is as if something were crumbling, decaying and exhausting itself, while something else, still indistinct, were arising from the rubble," Havel said. An eminent author as well as a post-Cold War statesman, Havel claims the modern age is over and we are in a transitional period that is distinguished by "mixing and blending of cultures and plurability or parallelism of intellectual and spiritual worlds. These are periods when all constant systems collapse, when cultures distant in time and space are discovered or rediscovered. New meaning is gradually born from the encounter, or the intersection, of many different elements."

The conflicts between nations are and will be more economic than political, and nation-states may well play a secondary role to the power of multi-national corporations without national allegiances. Although the United States currently is the only superpower, it is being challenged economically by Japan, Europe and an emerging China.

7

Nevertheless, America will be the major player on the world scene — whether it wishes so or not.

The world is badly fragmented with the break-up of the Soviet Union and of many states in Africa plus the emergence of an integrated South Africa reclaiming its rightful place on the world scene. Japan, China, Korea, and Taiwan are economic miracles with questionable political structures, while the Middle East remains an area of constant turmoil. Many leaders see a North-South split with the northern nations being the "haves" and the southern nations the "have nots" — a most dangerous situation in the long term.

All this turmoil and economic reshuffling could worsen as the population explosion continues in many undeveloped parts of the world. There will be populations craving for the food and the stability that are only available in the developed nations. Worldwide immigration from the "have not" nations to the "have" nations will be constant and is likely to quicken in pace over the years.

The world's population explosion will have a significant impact on all aspects of society over the next 25 to 50 years — probably longer. Today's population is estimated at 5.3 billion and by 2025 it will rise to an estimated 8.5 billion. The World Bank thinks population worldwide will stabilize in the second half of the 21st Century at between 10 and 11 billion — or maybe 14 billion. (Other forecasts are more conservative.) Most of the population growth, perhaps more than 90 percent, will be in the underdeveloped parts of the world. It is ironic that it is Western health practices — immunizations and antibiotics — that are primarily responsible for this population explosion. It could be, however, that AIDS could slow this growth if ways are not found to control the disease, as could birth control measures as we have seen in China.

This population explosion, as Prof. Paul Kennedy points out in his classic "Preparing for the Twenty-First Century," will "lead to social unrest, political instability and regional wars." Furthermore, the economic activity generated by this population explosion could "risk endangering the delicate envelope of matter that makes this planet unique," according to Prof. Kennedy. The population explosion will not be uniform. Indeed, in some parts of the world there will be population declines, particularly in the developed parts of the world. It is interesting to note that the world's population in 1825 was only one billion and it doubled by 1925 to two billion and doubled again to four billion by 1976.

Surely this population explosion will impact upon the global economy, upon the world's political stability, and upon the world's social structure to say nothing about the world's delicate environmental balances. The crucial question will be: can this small planet we call Earth feed and shelter so many people? At the same time, we may be entering a new industrial age — an automated age dominated by computers and robots — with vast implications for both the developed and undeveloped worlds. As always, we will have the classic race between population and technology.

There is the hope that technology can once again emerge quickly enough to provide the food and shelter these populations will require. But can the limited resources of our small planet sustain so many people, as our forests disappear, and as farmlands erode from overuse and undernourishment? There are some promising developments in bio-technology and other technologies, but will the developed world be willing to share them with the underdeveloped world? And could these underdeveloped nations find the capability to use the technology if it were made available?

This is a dangerous world with so many nations having the capability to build and deliver nuclear bombs. Nevertheless, hydrogen and nuclear bombs so far at least have served as a deterrent to warfare. One can only hope this will continue.

Meanwhile, America needs to find its way in a New World without a Cold War and without enduring ties to

Great Britain and to Europe, and with a more independent Japan, a stronger and perhaps militant China, and with a lessened superpower status. The nation already is finding it difficult to develop a strategy to survive in this New World. This situation could emerge as the issue of the next several decades, because it has no easy answers and as yet no creative theme.

At home, Americans must mend a changing economy — an economy running out of steam for lack of manufacturing enterprises. The nation must face up to the challenges of Japan, China, and other Asian states, of Europe no matter how divided, and of an emerging Russia with its vast national resources and highly educated population, and it must recognize that it will need to have a national strategy for economic war — whether we call it an industrial strategy or give it some other title. This war will be fought with research and development, an efficient manufacturing industry, and a highly educated, well-trained workforce. Currently, we are falling behind in all of these areas.

The nation also faces a huge trade deficit, which is permitting its assets to be taken over by foreign nations, foreign nationals, and multinational corporations, and a budget deficit that has nearly bankrupted the nation, preventing it from solving its economic and social problems and weakening its political institutions. Although the environment is a topic of much discussion, limited actions have been taken to preserve our air and water as environmentalists and industrialists jockey for advantage.

The nation will also need to cope with a diversity of ethnic groups that are large and growing — powerful and different — which will be reinforced over the years by immigrants from many nations fueled by the population explosion — attracted to America by the prospect of jobs and a better quality of life. There will be more immigrants no matter what policies and no matter what measures or steps are implemented. Immigration is as predictable as the next high tide.

The nation also faces social distress: an unprecedented wave of vicious crime, youth gangs that terrorize neighborhoods, homelessness involving entire families, and inadequate housing in our cities. Today, a third of all births and more than 60 percent of births in the Black community are to unwed mothers — most of whom are teenagers — which often leads to a vicious cycle of school drop outs, and generations of dependency on welfare and child abuse as well as a weakening of the entire social fabric. An attitude of vindictiveness abounds as society seeks security by tossing more and more criminals into jail — and too often into a lifelong career of crime. Most of the crimes involve illegal drug use, but efforts are limited to prevent the use of illegal drugs and to cure the drug abusers. Although Americans are living in an era of violence and fear, the nation continues to permit the sale to civilians of weapons larger and more powerful than those given to their law enforcement personnel.

Meanwhile, like the world economy, the domestic economy continues to further divide the nation into two camps: the rich and the poor or the "haves" and the "have nots." The middle class is being badly eroded. Increasingly those who are highly educated or well-trained for the workplace are doing well economically while those who are not highly educated or well-trained are not. This trend is growing and becoming ever more dangerous to the basic fabric of our society and could lead to social upheaval. The number of young people growing up in poverty continues to increase and little is being done to change these conditions.

Although all this seems very pessimistic, the nation is not without many strengths. For all its ills, the United States remains the most powerful, the most compassionate and the most democratic nation in the world as well as one of the richest with one of the highest standards of living. But all of this may not be good enough for a future of political unrest, foreign economic competition, and social disarray.

As America looks to the future, it must take a new and harder look at its entire educational system — a system that should be providing men and women who are prepared to meet the needs of a new, global economy; who appreciate the seriousness of our social ills; who understand our basic political structure and are prepared to participate as well-informed citizens, and who communicate, compute and think critically and make rational decisions. It must produce citizens who can live and work in a New World dominated by a global economy and by political instability.

America, once again, must believe it is safe to dream: to dream of an educational system that serves well nearly all children; to dream of a system of higher education, including a more comprehensive system of community colleges that serves its adults comprehensively and effectively; to dream that its social ills can be resolved for most of its citizens; to dream that peace and tranquility can again be a reality, and as "New York Times" columnist Bob Herbert wrote, to dream that "everything is possible, given enough time, enough effort and enough goodwill" and that "bad things could be made good and good things wonderful."

Part III

Creating A World-Class Educational System

A changing America within a changing world requires a world-class educational system at all levels. Unfortunately, we do not have one. America has some schools that are truly of world-class quality, turning out broadly educated young men and women who are prepared for higher education and for vital, high-paying positions within the workforce. Undoubtedly, many students do learn and do go on to successful careers in higher education or in the workforce. But for many young people — including some high school graduates — the American school system is a failure.

Most American school systems claim their goal is to serve all young people, but the truth is that they serve only some of them really well. Too many are not served well at all; far too many students drop out before they complete high school, and far too many high school graduates are not really broadly educated. Indeed, some who graduate are functionally illiterate. And far too many come out of high school having taken a general curriculum that fails to prepare them for further education or for employment. Whether we admit it or not, America's school system is a failure for many students. (Americans do not like to admit failure about anything and have yet to face up to this reality.)

A nation as rich as America should not have hundreds of thousands of its residents who are illiterate. In an emerging global economy, the illiterate job-seeker cannot find gainful

13

employment. Those kinds of jobs no longer exist. What happens to these people? They often become a hard-core segment of our welfare problem; they often become our unemployed or underemployed; they often become our homeless, and they often become involved in crime and drug abuse.

The break-up of the traditional family and the rise of families with two wage-earners has often produced parents who are more concerned about earning money than rearing and educating their children. Leave education to the schools and to the educators has been the refrain of some parents. But schools cannot provide an adequate education for most children without intensive, extensive and continuing support from parents. This is not happening in today's America and it is not likely to happen in tomorrow's America. And we have not yet invented a viable substitute.

The efforts to educate our children in America have been greatly hampered by television — an industry hungry for ratings and dollars no matter what the cost to society. Television has attracted millions of our young people to sit far too many hours in front of a screen watching programs with too much violence and sex, creating a world of unreality for many young people. TV has taken our young people away from relaxing and studying and homework; away from play and wholesome games and exercise; away from employment and away from parental influence and caring.

Just as damaging is the failure of our educational system to impart to our students often enough an understanding and appreciation for democracy. We have a citizenry today that is often politically illiterate, often uncaring about and essentially uninterested in the political process. This is caused to some degree by television programming that has failed in its responsibility to inform and arouse the public sufficiently to participate in the political enterprise. Democracy cannot long exist without well-informed, active participants who make rational decisions based on what is best for the entire society. The combination of an inadequate school system and an uncaring television industry has been devastating to the development of a responsible citizenry. They are often unprepared to vote intelligently, and are easily subjected to special interests or often do not care much about the entire enterprise. So few citizens vote today that most decisions are being made by a small minority of the total society.

The American school system is not only a failure for many young people as individuals, but it is the primary reason for many national problems. A good example is the "welfare problem." Anyone who has been close to this issue knows it is to a major degree an educational problem. Too many "dependent children" drop out of high school — often because of unwanted pregnancies — and become enmeshed within the welfare system from which they have great difficulty leaving because they are unprepared for gainful employment or for further education. Another example is our "crime problem" — a problem that often involves young people who are disenchanted by the school system and elect a career of crime rather than one of employment. Meanwhile, business and industry have been forced to spend millions of dollars each year to educate their employees, because the school system failed to do so adequately.

But the greatest embarrassment of all and the greatest failure of the American school system is the enormous number of adults who are illiterate. There is no official definition of illiteracy, but the National Literacy Act of 1991 used this definition:

> [An] Individual's ability to read, write and speak in
> English and compute and solve problems at levels
> of proficiency necessary to function on the job and
> in society.

These are people who cannot function well in a knowledge-based society that requires high educational levels. In the 1980s literacy was defined as the ability to read and write, but as we approach the year 2000 we need a broader definition that not only includes the ability to read and write but also the ability to speak, perform computations, solve problems, and use computers. Furthermore, literacy problems also include the growing number of individuals who have limited ability to speak, read, write or understand the English language. This number is expected to reach 17 million by the year 2000.

"Adult Literacy in America: A First Look at the Results of the National Adult Literacy Survey" presents the results of a survey funded by the U.S. Department of Education. Literacy was defined and measured by the National Adult Literacy Survey based on three scales reflecting varying degrees of skill in prose, document and cognitive literacy. It found that 21 to 23% of 191 million adults demonstrated skills in the lowest level of proficiency, Level 1, and 25 to 28% demonstrated skills at Level 2 proficiency. The Level 2 respondents did not consider themselves at risk and described themselves as able to read and write English "well" or "very well."

"Lower literacy levels positively correlated with lower levels of education and increasing age," the report said. "Higher levels of literacy were positively associated with employment, working more weeks in a year, and earning higher wages. Finally, nearly 50% of all adults in the lowest literacy level were living in poverty as compared with only 4% to 8% of those in the two highest proficiency levels."

Another report of the Department of Education was even more pessimistic. It claimed that half of our adults are functioning at a level of literacy below what is demanded by today's complex society. Imagine that! Half of our entire adult population lacking adequate literacy skills for today's society. And hardly anyone notices. It is tragic that so little is being done about the problem. Unfortunately, literacy for adults has never been given a high priority in America even though data show literacy instruction produces positive results. Programs that are very intensive for extensive periods of time have the best chance for success. Nevertheless, the lives of many adults would be greatly enriched through improved literacy skills, and the nation's future security would be substantially improved by the development of an expanded workforce with the ability to perform in a complex global economy.

Educators have been hoping for the past decade that graduates of American high schools would at least improve in the basic skills of reading, writing and arithmetic. But data from the former New Jersey Department of Higher Education on its Collegiate Basic Skills Placement Test show otherwise. In 1994, the Department reported that incoming freshmen had not improved their verbal and mathematics scores for the fifteenth consecutive year. The test results are appalling. They show that only 22.4 percent of the new college freshmen in New Jersey are proficient in verbal skills, 32 percent in basic mathematics, and only 13.6 percent in algebra. Furthermore, the federal Department of Education reported in December, 1993 that American eighth graders are being out-performed in mathematics by their counterparts in other industrialized nations. Outperforming American students were their counterparts in Taiwan, South Korea, Switzerland, the former Soviet Union, Hungary, France, Israel, Canada, Slovenia, Ireland and Scotland. Only Jordan's students performed below those of Americans.

Economists often speak of a new world of the "haves" and the "have nots" based on income levels. But the truth is that we really have a society of "haves" and "have nots" based on educational achievement. Those who are well-educated achieve the good life and those without an education live in or close to poverty levels and often in despair.

Although education reform is much talked about, it has been little more than talk. No fundamental changes have been made although many successful pilot programs abound. The educational system and the educators are not totally to blame for our educational crisis. Many Americans need to point to themselves for failing to help educate their children or even to be much concerned about their education; for failing to demand competent, productive schools, and for often failing to provide adequate resources.

Dealing with this educational crisis on a national level is difficult because of our decentralized system of public education. America does not really have a national educational system. At best, it has 50 separate systems. Even that may not be true. There are thousands of local school districts. In New Jersey, for example, there are more than 600 school districts (some that do not even have a school) serving 1.1 million students. (The State spends $600 million annually just for superintendents of schools and we see few if any of them in the classroom.) In many states, local school systems are very independent and uncoordinated. These local school systems have local goals that may or may not meet national needs — particularly the needs of a changing America within a changing world. Historically and traditionally, education has been a service that has been delegated to the states. Perhaps it would be more accurate to say that education is a service claimed by the states and retained with great vigor. The national role has been primarily collecting data, providing a few dollars and staying out of the way. Until the end of World War II, this arrangement had been adequate. Of course, some states did a better job than others, but the needs of business and industry were met and the needs of society were served. But we can no longer say that. The needs of society and of business and industry are not being met adequately.

"Paying Attention to the Schools Is A National Mission Now" was the headline in "The Week in Review" section of the "New York Times" on October 1, 1989 (if only it were true). It referred to President Bush's so-called "education summit." It is noteworthy that President Clinton (then governor of Arkansas) said, "This is the first time in the history of the country that we have ever thought enough of education to commit ourselves to national performance goals." Out of the "summit" came national goals that address dropout rates, literacy, teacher quality, drugs and physical readiness of kindergartners to learn.

In 1983, "A Nation at Risk" report was prepared by the National Commission on Excellence in Education. It deplored the "rising tide of mediocrity" in the schools and called for tougher high school graduation requirements, more core academic courses, higher teacher salaries and other measures. Of course, other alarms had been sounded some 30 years earlier when the Soviet Union launched "Sputnik" and frightened Washington into increasing support for science and mathematics education. But the system today is no better — perhaps worse. And still there is no outcry from the public to do much about it. The nation is still at risk — only the risk is greater.

It was the Census Bureau in 1995 that conducted a survey that makes the best case for educational reform in America. It found that employers express a lack of confidence in the ability of schools and colleges to prepare young people for the workplace. (The study, it should be noted, was produced for the federal Department of Education.) The study also found that employers report that one-fifth of their workers are not fully proficient in their jobs; that in selecting workers they disregarded grades and school evaluations and relied more on job applicant's attitude, behavior and job experience, and that they no longer hired students straight out of school. And, the study found, employers were more likely to hire equipment suppliers or private consultants to train their employees rather than educational institutions. The study also found that employers see an increasing level of skills being needed in the workplace; that two of five production and non-supervisory employees used computers in their jobs, and that 81 percent of them reported paying for or providing some form of formal training to workers.

If America is to reform or to reinvent its school system, there are items that need to be considered. These would include much greater parental involvement in the whole educational process; greater emphasis on parent education; more attention to pre-school education; more time spent on academic subjects throughout the entire educational spectrum from pre-school to higher education; smaller administrative components if not smaller schools and colleges; more professional teachers who believe that nearly all children can learn; after-school and evening programs for children and adults; emphasis on instructional personnel and a deemphasis on administrative and other personnel; more pre-college activities involving school systems and institutions of higher education; a longer school day and a longer school year; increased emphasis on academics and reduced emphasis on athletics and student activities; much greater flexibility within the whole system, and recognizing that children learn in different ways and at different speeds.

But the key to all reform is the parents. They must appreciate the value of education; must play an active role in educating their children; must support the whole educational enterprise, both politically and financially, and must demand that society provides schools where nearly all children learn to the point where graduates can function well in a modern, civilized world and a democratic society. The parents must demand from their political leaders and their educational leaders an educational system that works for America — and works very well.

Parents must feel an obligation to form a partnership with the educational system to educate their children. Parents can be more useful than they realize by reading to their children, by helping their children with their homework (perhaps even learning together), by providing them cultural activities; by encouraging them to learn (especially to read and write), and by helping them develop confidence that they can learn, and by instilling in them an appreciation that learning can be fun as well as useful in future life. Parents need to forge a partnership with their children's teachers and work as a team to develop the full potential of every child. This will, of course, require increased training for both parents and teachers, so they understand each others' role and complement each others' efforts. Although this kind of dialogue is rare, it should be happening often and continuously as the child moves through the educational continuum. Citizens must become advocates for an educational system from pre-school to post-doctoral levels. And when they have the opportunity, they must vote for education and for the resources to make it happen.

Society must recognize that America's family structure is disintegrating. And educators must find ways to compensate for the absence of parents in the homes of many young people. Schools cannot do everything, but some efforts can be useful. One such component would be after-school and evening centers for children with no place to go after school or in the evening. There could be community centers with educational and recreational services for young people as well as their parents and other adults (a role community colleges might well serve). These centers could include Learning Centers and tutoring as well as some classroom instruction. (They provide another way to bring parents and schools closer together to forge stronger partnerships.)

America must take a step back and ask itself: what does it take to have a world-class educational system? What does it take to develop an educational system in which nearly all children learn? Only then can it begin to take steps to make this happen. Clearly, the current system is inadequate and deteriorating. America will fail as a nation and a world power if it does not quickly realize that its educational system is inadequate for a New World of the 21st Century. America must take steps quickly to reinvent or at least reinvigorate the entire educational enterprise.

America must begin to acknowledge the linkages between an inadequate educational system with many of its social ills, crime, welfare dependency, and a lack of economic competitiveness in the world. Once these connections are made, America will face up to the problem and will really do something about it — making major changes in its educational system. Then it will give education the priority it deserves. These changes must include a massive, comprehensive program to combat illiteracy. It would be the least expensive way to fight many social problems and it would begin to develop a literate workforce with the ability to be upgraded and retrained to meet the emerging needs of a global economy. To resolve this will require a nationwide effort with major fiscal support from the federal government. Furthermore, far more attention must be given to the "quiet crisis," as former New Jersey Gov. Tom Kean put it, to our neglect of young children. Perhaps we need a Head Start program for many more children, after-school activities for young people who are left unattended while their parents work, a longer school day and a longer school year, and vastly improved ways to teach the basics of reading, writing, speaking and computing for all students.

The American educational system is not working for far too many students and it is not working for a declining America — a decline that can be traced to the educational system as much as to any other segment of society. It is a decline that can only be reversed by invigorating our entire educational system. America's number one problem, therefore, is a failing school system. Not only because the school system is a failure for so many people, but because those failures are the root cause of so many other problems. Much of our social decay can be traced directly to the lack of a truly effective educational system.

Because of its strategic position, its accessibility, and its record of success, it is the community college that is geared to play a leading role in a campaign to reinvent the American educational system. It has strong ties to both the elementary and secondary schools and to other institutions of higher education. It articulates with both and it has partnerships and cooperative efforts with both. It can and must be the link with both sectors to help develop a new, more successful American educational system. The community college movement must help create a world-class educational system for America to serve a changing nation within a changing world.

Part IV

Today's System of Higher Education

The American system of higher education is broad, diverse and vast, serving some 12 million undergraduates, thousands more doing graduate work, and thousands more in continuing education offerings. The system is comprised of great research universities, major state universities and colleges, four-year liberal arts colleges, specialized colleges and universities in such fields as engineering, medicine, education and religion, two-year technical institutes, two-year junior colleges, and two-year community colleges, as well as a few men's and women's colleges. Altogether, the United States has 3,716 institutions of higher education. There are 2,149 four-year colleges and universities — 1,551 private and 598 public. Within this vast network, the community colleges represent about 40 percent of the institutions and 43 percent of the total undergraduate enrollment. They are the growth area of higher education today.

By philosophy and mission, most — if not all — four-year colleges have a specific role that is not intended to be comprehensive. Some offer only liberal arts, while others offer a limited number of programs. By design, most four-year colleges limit their enrollment. They often claim to be selective in their admissions and often limit the number of students overall and by program. Many are reluctant to admit those other than immediate high school graduates and some do not accept part-time students. But these attitudes are changing as many four-year colleges have found adults in their 20s and 30s to be highly motivated students — whether they attend full-time or part-time. The major universities are comprehensive in nature programatically, but they too practice selective admissions and place limits on enrollment.

Most four-year colleges are geared to serve a very wide constituency, sometimes just statewide but often across several states or an entire region. Many recruit students nationwide or by regions such as the Southwest or Northeast. They do not have distinct service areas, as community colleges do.

The general public often makes the unrealistic assumption that all four-year colleges or universities perform at high levels of excellence. Such is not the case. There are great four-year colleges and universities and there are those that are not so great. But even at our great research universities, we sometimes find poor undergraduate instruction (just ask a few graduates). And too often graduate assistants or graduate students are the instructors for freshman and sophomore courses. Many community college transfer students will tell you (as they have often told me) that the best instruction they have ever received was at the community college rather than at their prestigious four-year college or university.

There is, of course, competition in higher education. Institutions are always vying for students, for programs, and especially for funds regardless of the source. This competition is intense and keen, as it should be. The competition is not only between institutions, but is also between types of institutions.

At the same time, there is considerable and increasing cooperation and collaboration between and among institutions of higher education. In the current period of limited resources, colleges and universities are finding they can do more for less by working together, making better use of fiscal and human resources. These collaborations include all sectors of higher education and the partnerships are between and among all sectors: universities with community colleges, community colleges with independent institutions, and state colleges with technical institutes among others.

Although many community college students transfer to four-year colleges and universities, America's four-year institutions hardly know community colleges exist. That includes chief executive officers, faculty and staff. And admissions offices do not know too much about them either. Community colleges are where the action is today, but few four-year institutions are aware of their growth, their broad-based programs or their impact upon local communities. Many four-year college and university leaders still think the community college is in some other domain separate and apart from them. They fail to realize the impact community colleges have made and are making on society — and on higher education. The growth and impact of community colleges are almost a secret to the general public and to the other sectors of higher education.

Each sector of higher education has its role to play and each contributes to a total system of higher education that is the envy of the entire world. Each sector is important to the system's total impact on society and it is imperative that all sectors be nourished and further enriched as they will be ever more important to the world of the future.

But it is the community college that:

- is close to the people;
- understands the needs of its service area and the people who live there;
- is flexible, serving full-time and part-time students, matriculated and non-matriculated students, and daytime, evening and weekend students;
- is service-oriented with talented, experienced providers of community services;
- is experienced in serving adults, including senior citizens, minorities, educationally and economically disadvantaged and the under-

> prepared (or even unprepared, or "at-risk") students;
> - is experienced and productive in conducting successful developmental studies programs;
> - has faculties dedicated to teaching;
> - has vast, broad-based student support services for all segments of their student bodies, and
> - is affordable.

Of course, all colleges and universities have some of these components as well, but no other sector has all of them. None is as close to its constituents or as knowledgeable about their needs as the community college. Therefore, community colleges are well positioned to meet the specific needs of their service area.

The community college is the only sector of higher education that can effectively, economically and immediately carry out national educational goals at the local level. They have all the components available to do it successfully, providing they obtain adequate additional funding from the federal government. For a changing America within a changing world, the community college movement can begin to help solve some of the nation's fundamental woes such as illiteracy, an underdeveloped workforce, an ill-informed, uninterested citizenry, and an educational system in need of major reform. What needs to be done is to fully utilize the network of the 1,200 regionally-accredited community colleges.

Part V

Today's Community College

The community college movement in America today is extensive. Its growth has been dynamic — even spectacular. The movement includes nearly 1,500 institutions that serve more than 11 million students: 6.5 million seeking an academic credential and about 5 million more in all other academic activities such as continuing education. Today they enroll more than half of all the first time freshmen who are in an institution of higher education in the country. There are community colleges in every state, in every Congressional district, in almost every major population center, and in urban, suburban and rural areas. Community colleges come in all sizes from a few hundred students to more than 100,000 students and in many types. (A community college is defined by the American Association of Community Colleges as an institution that is regionally accredited and the associate degree is the highest conferred.)

The two-year college in America has a number of configurations. Some are church-related and private and often called junior colleges, but other junior colleges are not church-related and serve single or limited missions. Some are technical institutes with a vocational focus. But most of them are comprehensive community colleges with extensive transfer, career, developmental and community services functions, extensive student support services and open door admissions policies. They are the growth area of the two-year college movement.

The National Center for Education Statistics listed 1,469 two-year institutions of higher education in 1992-93 — 1,024 public and 445 private. According to the Center, California had the largest number of two-year colleges, 144, while New York was second with 95, including 49 private institutions (the largest number of private two-year colleges in the nation). Rhode Island has only one two-year college, while Alaska and South Dakota have only two and Delaware only three. Other states with a large number of two-year colleges include: Texas 79, Ohio and Pennsylvania 72 each, North Carolina 67, Illinois 66, Georgia 65, Minnesota 54 and Florida 45. More than half of the 1,469 two-year colleges are located in these ten states. The annual survey of the American Association of Community Colleges in 1992-93 listed 1,158 community colleges: 975 public and 183 private. Fifty years earlier, the Association listed only 648 two-year colleges and more than half of them were private: 315 public and 333 private.

About a fourth of all public community colleges enroll 6,000 students or more; another fourth between 3,000 and 6,000; another fourth between 1,500 and 3,000, and the remainder of 1,500 or less. The private institutions are much smaller. Only 25 percent of them have more than 1,000 students, while another 25 percent have 400 or fewer students. Some of these comprehensive community colleges are very large indeed. Miami-Dade in Florida, for example, operates on five campuses and serves about 55,000 students. And the gigantic Los Angeles Community College System serves 117,000 students.

The community college movement is about 100 years old. The movement has no official starting date — as do many colleges — but it traces its beginnings to 1882 at the University of Chicago. Writing in the "Community College Times," James Wattenbarger and Allen Witt said:

> The slim historical literature that exists presents an uneven and often contradictory picture of the movement. Various authors credit the universities of Michigan, Georgia, Minnesota

and Chicago with starting the movement.

But Wattenbarger and Witt add:

> The birthplace of this movement was the University of Chicago. Its founder was the university's first president, a young scholar named William Rainey Harper. In the nine years following 1882, Harper was directly responsible for creating the associate degree, the first public junior college and the beginnings of a nation-wide movement.

The junior college was fashioned as a two-year institution designed primarily to provide the first two years of the standard four-year college curriculum. They were mostly independent institutions and they concentrated on transferring their students with advanced standing to four-year colleges and universities. Joliet Junior College in Joliet, Ill., claims to be the oldest. It was started as an off-shoot of the University of Chicago in 1901.

In the late '50s following the success of the GI Bill, a national movement developed to provide higher education for all rather than for a privileged few — a movement driven by the establishment of the comprehensive community colleges. These comprehensive community colleges not only provided the traditional transfer programs, but also career programs designed to meet the demands for workers with skills to handle the new technologies — particularly skills appropriate to the needs of local business and industry. Community colleges had their greatest enrollment increases between 1965 and 1975 — up 215 percent from 1,292,000 to 4,069,000. (During a portion of that period, a new community college was opened on average every week.) The community college movement broadened still further with the addition of a community services component designed especially for the areas they served. These services were in such areas as economic development, workforce development (jobs training, for example), cultural offerings and recreational activities. These were augmented by a wide variety of continuing education programs that also were community-oriented.

Community colleges are affordable for students. Tuition and fees are low — usually the lowest of any institution of higher education in the area they serve. Public community colleges have low tuition because they receive funds from public sources, usually state and county appropriations, and their operating costs are lower than four-year colleges. Furthermore, extensive financial aid is available in the form of federal and state grants and loans and private scholarships. Some community colleges have even developed financial aid packages for part-time students. And many community colleges have large work-study programs and often are involved in cooperative education programs that provide modest wages for students.

During periods of rapid growth in the college-age population, community colleges were often started "as a less expensive, alternate method to educate freshman and sophomore students," James L. Wattenbarger, distinguished service professor and director for the Institute of Higher Education, College of Education, University of Florida, said in his "Community College Financing 1990: Challenges for A New Decade." Over the years, community colleges have been in the position of being the last established and the last funded by the states. The states fund their K-12 systems first, the university-state college system next and the community colleges last. Many states depend upon income and sales tax for most of their funding for their community colleges, but there is a trend for states also to use lottery and excise taxes on cigarettes and alcohol to fund them.

"Community colleges are low-cost institutions when compared to public and private four-year programs," Wattenbarger reported. In most states, this has resulted in a dual pricing system: the high-priced four-year program and the low-priced two-year system.

State support for community colleges ranges from 100 percent in Hawaii to Wisconsin's 25 percent. Overall, state aid is about 58 percent of the revenues of community colleges, while local support is about 13 percent, tuition and fees about 22 percent, (but this is increasing and a larger percent is being borne by students through tuition and fees — which in the long run will surely compromise accessibility and affordability), federal aid less than three percent and other revenues (gifts, endowment revenue, and grants) about four percent. New Hampshire expends the most dollars per full-time equivalent student ($6,827) for its community colleges and another New England state, Vermont, the least ($2,706). The average is about $3,900.

The mission statements of community colleges are quite similar. They almost always contain a commitment to the transfer or university-parallel function (meaning students can transfer with advanced standing to a four-year college or university), to career programs (designed primarily to provide immediate employment upon graduation), to developmental and remedial studies (designed to prepare students for college-level work), to continuing education and lifelong learning and community services offerings. They also include extensive student support services as well as a commitment to open admissions and to affordability. What's important to know, however, is the emphasis given to each of these components — based on the needs of the constituency the institution serves.

As open admissions institutions, community colleges provide higher educational opportunities for all adults within the area they serve — or at least all adults who can benefit from their instruction. This includes those immediately out of high school to those who are senior citizens — and all the ages in between; those at all educational levels; those from all ethnic and religious backgrounds, and those from all income levels.

Community colleges are open to all adults. This means they are accepted into the institution, but they must qualify for entry into a particular program. If they cannot meet the entrance requirements into a program, the institution provides courses for them to qualify. Developmental and remedial classes in the basic skills, or English for speakers of other languages or high school level courses in such areas as biology, chemistry or physics or the social sciences and others are offered. This is how the open admissions policy should really work: admit everyone to the institution, but allow no one to take a college credit course until he or she is prepared to benefit from the instruction. This is no easy task, because students are very creative in finding ways to bypass developmental studies courses, which usually provide no credit.

Community colleges are attractive to many students — both young and old — because of their flexibility. (About 13 percent of the full-time students are older than 30 and 48 percent are younger than 21, while 34 percent of the part-time students are older than 30 and 16 percent are younger than 21.) Students can usually attend on a full-time or part-time basis (64 percent of all community college students attend part-time.) Over the past decade, enrollment of part-time students grew three times as fast as those attending full-time, (taking classes in the daytime, in the evening or on weekends usually at any time that best fits their own schedules), and as majors or non-majors. This flexibility is particularly important for those who must work while attending college and for those who have other personal and family responsibilities. Community colleges are open to all — from those who are very well prepared for college and wish to begin their college careers at their hometown community college to those who are ill-prepared — really unprepared — for college.

More minority students in America — 55 percent — attend community colleges than any other type of institution of higher education, representing about 25 percent of all students enrolled in community colleges. Of the minority students in community colleges, 45 percent are African-American, 35 percent Hispanic; 18 percent Asian/Pacific Islander, and five percent American Indian. The urban areas are served more directly and more comprehensively by the community college than any other segment of higher education. For most economically disadvantaged students, community colleges are their best — and often their only —

hope of leaving the poverty in which they live. And for many minority students — except for outstanding athletes and a few outstanding scholars — the community college represents their only opportunity to benefit from the services of higher education. If community colleges did nothing else but serve minority and disadvantaged students successfully, they still would be a great asset to this nation. Obviously, they do much more. And in the future they will be asked to serve more economically and educationally disadvantaged students, more minority students, and more students from urban America — perhaps the greatest challenge facing tomorrow's community college.

Proximity is another attraction for many students to attend community colleges. Many community colleges are located in urban centers and in the suburbs. To make college more accessible, some community colleges have two or three or as many as five campuses to serve students' needs — as well as off-campus sites in local high schools, industrial plants, hospitals and community centers.

Another attraction for many students is the community colleges' emphasis on teaching and learning. Professors primarily teach, although a few publish and do research, and they mentor and advise students as additional student support services. And today's community college is in the forefront of using technology for academic purposes.

Perhaps most attractive to students is the wide variety of programs most community colleges offer, ranging from the arts and sciences to the technologies. They usually offer both two-year programs leading to an Associate Degree and short-term programs leading to a certificate or a diploma. Most community colleges have many offerings in the business and commerce areas. In the business area, many community colleges have programs in accounting, banking, insurance, real estate, business administration, marketing, office systems technologies, and telecommunications — to list a few. Computer science is a major emphasis of most community colleges. In the health services area, community colleges offer programs in dental hygiene, medical record technology, nursing, ophthalmic assistant technology, physical therapy assistant and radiologic technology. The engineering technologies are popular with many community colleges offering such programs as manufacturing, automotive, chemical, civil, construction, electrical, electro-mechanical, machine tool and mechanical technology. For the agricultural business, community colleges provide such programs in agricultural science, agronomy and animal husbandry. Public service-related programs are often available in child care, criminal justice, early childhood education, fire protection technology, human services, park and recreation management and security administration. And there are hundreds more.

Community colleges frequently offer programs geared specifically to the needs of their constituents: transportation and distribution management, apparel production management, textile management, wine merchandising, jewelry design, leather accessory design and production, aerospace technology, agriculture engineering technology, leather technology, marine technology, and textile technology, for example. Atlantic County Community College in New Jersey has a culinary arts program to serve the needs of the gambling casinos on the Atlantic City boardwalk as well as a program to train croupiers to run the betting tables.

Another attraction of the community college is the wide variety and types of offerings in continuing education or lifelong learning. This is a large segment of the community college's operations and one that is growing. Continuing education provides the community college the ability to offer courses, workshops and seminars in many disciplines — even in areas in which they do not offer a degree — and in many forms, ranging from a one-day seminar to a year-long non-credit certificate program. These offerings are often related to new careers or to helping students prepare better for existing careers. Continuing education and community service offerings are often those that do not fit neatly into a degree-granting category. They are designed to assist individuals to develop personal interests and capabilities — for credit or non-credit. These offerings are as broad and extensive as the creativity and imagination — and the availability of resources — will permit. Many community colleges are giving continuing education and community service offerings a new, deeper look, because they are often revenue-producing. Today's Continuing Education Departments often administer workforce development efforts, pre-college programs, College for Kids programs, senior citizen programs and other activities not assigned to the offices of academic affairs. They are growing in size and scope and taking on an ever more important role and higher priority in many community colleges. In many respects, they represent the cutting edge of the community college philosophy to serve all segments of society.

Many community colleges also provide customized training for businesses and industries — designing courses to meet the specific needs of a particular company. Some of these offerings can be as sophisticated as training General Motors' workers to operate and maintain robots, while many of the offerings are in the area of basic skills and ESL (English as a second language) courses or acute care assistant training for hospitals or Spanish or other languages for the import/export industries. Very often today they involve computer science courses of some kind.

Community colleges offer a wide variety of community services. Many specialize in cultural arts offerings; others in recreation activities or programs of personal enrichment. Working with local agencies involved in economic development (customized training, for example) is another community service for some community colleges. Usually these community services reflect the area and the constituency the community college serves. The community service segment of the community college's mission really developed on the back of President Lyndon Johnson's War on Poverty. In this atmosphere, many community colleges found that there were numerous ways in which they could serve the community more comprehensively and that they had many human and physical resources to make available.

Another feature of the community college is the extensive student support services they provide — all kinds of counseling, placement services and academic advisement, tutoring and extensive student activities. Unlike secondary schools, these student support services are offered outside of classroom time and not at the expense of instruction. These services are usually available to all students: day and evening, full-time and part-time, young and old. These services are crucial for many of the so-called non-traditional students (they really are the majority on community college campuses these days) — particularly the educationally and economically disadvantaged students. Intercollegiate athletics is a low-priority student activity at many community colleges, but not at all. Some take intercollegiate athletics very seriously — just like their four-year college colleagues. Hudson Valley Community College in Troy, N.Y., for example, is "big time" into football, boasting about its recruitment prowess and its ability to transfer gridders to four-year colleges who then go on to the pros. Others indulge in the same efforts in basketball, baseball and other sports.

Community colleges are everywhere and nowhere are they more prevalent than in California, which is the most community college-oriented state in the nation. The vast community college system in California enrolls 5.9 percent of all residents 18 and older — the highest penetration rate of any state. (The lowest penetration rate is in Louisiana where only .7 percent of the population 18 and older enroll in community colleges.) California's 107 community colleges enroll 1.3 million students, and the California Postsecondary Education Commission projects there will be a need for an additional 23 campuses by 2005 to serve about 540,000 additional students — an increase of 40 percent. A number of large metropolitan areas operate multi-college systems with the largest being the Los Angeles Community College. Six of the ten largest multi-college systems are in California. Nine of the ten largest single campus colleges are in California. The largest is City Colleges of San Francisco with 34,000 students. Breaking into the "top ten" along with the California entries is Broward Community College in Florida, which ranks eighth with 24,000 students. Miami-Dade Community College in Florida is the largest multi-campus college. Other large multi-campus colleges include: Houston Community College; Northern Virginia; St. Louis, Missouri; Macomb, Michigan; College of DuPage, Illinois; IVY-Tech, No. Dakota; Pima County, Arizona; Oakland, Michigan, and Tarrant County, Texas, all enrolling between 28,000 and 38,000 students.

In the past, a number of community colleges began in local high schools or abandoned industrial plants, but today's community colleges feature outstanding campuses with modern, attractive buildings and highly specialized facilities such as laboratories and clinics for their comprehensive programs. New York state proclaims, for example, that it offers the "majestic beauty of Clinton Community College housed in an old chateau overlooking Lake Champlain." Today we find community colleges located on former golf courses and farmlands, while others utilize former military installations or former office buildings. There are single-building campuses in major urban areas and there are multi-building campuses on large, open campuses of hundreds of acres. The campuses often reflect the community the institution serves, both in design and character.

The governance of community colleges varies greatly from state to state. For the nation's public community colleges, there are more than 600 Boards of Trustees. Most Board members are volunteers who serve without compensation (except for the satisfaction of seeing an institution grow and develop and serve the needs of so many people needing higher educational services).

In 21 states, community colleges are governed by a state board, while in 28 other states they are governed by local boards (15 are elected and 13 are appointed). In Alaska, Colorado, Georgia and New York, some community colleges are governed by a state board and others by local boards.

The growth of America's community college movement has been spectacular, but with this growth has come deficiencies. Far too many students fail to achieve their personal academic goal whether it be the successful completion of an associate degree, a certificate, a diploma, a group of courses, or a single course. Far too many graduates fail to transfer to four-year colleges and universities and far too many fail to get placed in good paying jobs.

Although comprehensive programming is one of the gems of the community college movement, too often there has been a proliferation of programs — some unneeded. Too often community colleges have developed a program simply because a neighboring institution had it. Too often community colleges have attempted to do too much with too little with a negative impact upon the students. For example, many community colleges have not had the resources to provide adequate student support services for the kinds of students they enrolled. There simply were inadequate resources to do the job well, but it was attempted anyway.

It is unfortunate that too many community colleges utilize far too many adjunct or part-time faculty. While adjuncts are very valuable to teach specialized courses in which they have expertise, an institution of higher education must have faculty who devote their careers to the institution — the backbone of the institution. These full-time faculty members must not only teach extensively, but must mentor students, maintain academic standards and develop and monitor curriculums. These tasks are seldom taken on by adjuncts.

Furthermore, in far too many community colleges a secondary school atmosphere is pervasive rather than an attitude of higher education. This makes the community college simply the thirteenth and fourteenth year of high school rather than the first two years of higher education.

Despite these deficiences, the community college movement has come a long way in the past century. But as America approaches the 21st Century it will require a broader, an even more comprehensive system of community colleges — community colleges geared to help solve national issues produced by an unsettled world and a global economy and to serve their specific constituents more comprehensively with excellence.

Part VI

The Emerging Community College Mission

A. Introduction

The New World of the 21st Century will require a more broadly educated and more literate citizen; a more highly trained workforce and often a retrained workforce; a more politically sophisticated citizen, and a truly broad-based lifelong learning mechanism for all men and women. With America changing within a changing world, the United States will need a "new" community college movement: one that is larger, broader, more comprehensive and of higher quality. Tomorrow's community colleges will need to do more and do it better. And they must do it for all segments of a more diverse population, including those of all ethnic backgrounds, of all religious affiliations, of all income levels and of all educational achievement levels. This will require a broader mission statement and more targeted goals and objectives for each community college. Each must be designed to meet the very specific needs of its constituency as well as the needs of a changing nation attempting to find its way in a changing world and in a menacing but potentially rich global economy.

Furthermore, the vast American community college movement should be part of a national effort to reinvigorate or reinvent the American educational system. The community college should take a leadership role in this crusade, since it has close ties to both the elementary and secondary schools and to the other institutions of higher education.

What then does a changing America within a changing world mean for the nations's community college movement? It means the movement must help provide:

1.   **A more broadly educated society;**
2.   **A more competent and more adaptable workforce;**
3.   **A more involved and better informed citizenry, and**
4.   **A broader, more comprehensive system of lifelong learning.**

Although many new avenues of opportunity will be opening up to community colleges, these institutions must always understand that they cannot be all things to all people. There will never be enough funds to do everything a community college might do well. Choices must always be made. Community colleges must select the activities with the highest priority, with the greatest need and with the greatest benefit to their constituents.

Community colleges should not only be concerned about a broader and more difficult mission, but also how to provide its services at a higher quality level — at quality levels that enable more students to reach their individual educational goals and potential whether it be a single course for personal enrichment, a number of courses or a one-year or two-year credential. What is needed is a higher "graduation rate" and a corresponding lower dropout rate for all of these goals. In assessing these graduation and attrition rates, it must be understood that many students drop out for non-academic reasons such as illness, changing employment and family responsibilities. Community colleges need to do a better job of determining these factors and evaluating the real reasons students do not reach their particular educational goal.

The faculties need to be better prepared academically and psychologically to teach a vastly different student body. In all likelihood, however, there will be extensive differences in the compositions of the faculty and the student body at many community colleges. Staff development designed to help faculty understand the cultures and mores of these students will be essential. Community colleges should reappraise continuously their student support services to determine if they are adequate and appropriate for the existing student body. This will be more necessary in the future as many community colleges recruit more diverse and older student bodies which will probably be less prepared for the college experience.

This means the mission, goals and objectives of every community college will be different. It also means that each institution should look at itself strategically to determine the needs of its constituents, to determine its competitors for funds, students and programs, and to determine what resources it has and can get to carry out its mission, goals and objectives. It is easy to set out the basic mission of the institution in most instances, particularly for the comprehensive community college. Establishing goals and objectives is the difficult part, because they must be geared specifically to the area the institution serves — needs that are not always obvious.

To meet the needs of a changing America within a changing world, community colleges will need to expand their mission statements to provide for a more broadly educated society, a more competent and more adaptable workforce, a more involved and better-informed citizenry, and a broader, more comprehensive system of lifelong learning and to be part of a national effort to reinvent the American educational system.

B. A More Broadly Educated Society

Education is geared to prepare students to live in an increasingly more complex and more disruptive world — a world that is changing faster than we can comprehend it. It is a world dominated by deteriorating political systems, by globalization of the economic system and by social unrest. But also a world with an information system that transmits data around the world in minutes.

All this speaks to the need for broadly educated men and women who can digest and analyze these changes, draw implications from them, and develop rational answers. That's what the jobs of the future will require. This demands that community colleges place an ever-greater emphasis upon general education courses for all students — deeper and broader studies in the arts and sciences and the humanities. Students must be better prepared to express themselves effectively, to think analytically, critically and reflectively, to be aware of themselves and the environment in which they live, to appreciate diverse cultures and to be morally and socially responsible citizens in our democratic society.

As the Wingspread Group on Higher Education stated in its "An American Imperative: Higher Expectations for Higher Education":

> For without a broad liberal education, students are denied the opportunity to engage with the principal ideas and events that are the source of any civilization. How then are they to understand values that sustain community and society, much less their own values.

This is, of course, no easy task. But it should be a goal and it should be the number one goal of every institution of higher education — two years or four years. As the world becomes ever more complex and as knowledge continues to explode, the need for the broadly educated person will increase exponentially. Therefore, community colleges will need to give greater emphasis to the arts and sciences — to develop more broadly educated men and women who know how to learn and how to make use of new knowledge as it becomes available. General education courses are always part of community college transfer programs, but now and in the future they will need to be emphasized to a greater degree. Even lifelong learning efforts need to offer studies that might be considered part of the liberal arts.

This also speaks to teaching students how to learn — bibliographic studies, for example. Greater emphasis will need to be given to the use of the library as a resource for knowledge. Many people could learn a great deal on their own about the new global economy, for example, using the vast resources of their local libraries, (as well as their local community college library) including the use of on-line informational services. But how many students today — high school or college — know how to use a library? Too few, no doubt.

"The old work ethic of everyone grinding away won't keep American companies competitive," according to Ruth Brennan, director of human resources of Bic Corp., Milford, CN., who added that she seeks in even entry-level employees "smarts, speed, flexibility, the ability to handle risk and ambiguity, knowing how to find out what you don't know and how to teach others what you do know." Many in business and industry today share her views.

Speaking of a broadly educated student body is difficult for community colleges when so many students enter vastly unprepared for the college experience — some of them virtually functionally illiterate. This does not imply that they cannot learn. It simply states the fact of their educational achievement. This lack of achievement is often not of their making, but simply the circumstances in which they grew up.

Before the community college can help develop a more broadly educated society, it must first produce many more literate men and women – men and women with the basic skills of reading, writing and arithmetic necessary for all learning. In addition, community colleges in the future will need to add a new basic skill: computer literacy. Students will need to be computer literate to use the wide variety of computer-assisted instruction tools available at many community and other colleges. And many — if not all — jobs in the future will require some knowledge of computers. The community college student must have these skills in the world of the 21st century.

Businesses need people who understand that information is a competitive advantage and who are comfortable with gathering and using it, William C. Ferguson, president and chief executive officer of NYNEX, said. "Whether the employee is an inventory clerk at a Wal-Mart store or a bond trader on Wall Street or a teacher, getting the right information in front of the right people to be used in the right way is going to make the difference between winning and losing in the global economy."

Most community colleges have extensive developmental studies programs in the basic skills and many offer high school level courses in many disciplines for students who did not take them earlier. As the data show, it is likely most of America's community colleges will need to do more than ever before in the area of developmental studies. There will be more unprepared and underprepared recent high school graduates and other adults. And there will be more — many more — immigrants needing to learn English, if nothing else. In areas with high numbers of immigrants (both legal and illegal) there will be an ever-increasing need for courses in English for speakers of other languages. And there will be an extensive need for Adult Basic Education and GED (high school equivalency) preparatory courses.

Illiteracy is a monumental national problem — a problem mostly ignored and a problem getting worse rather than better. And it will be the community college upon which the burden will fall to resolve it — simply because there are few other agencies large enough and broad enough to cope successfully with it. The illiteracy problem is particularly critical in our urban areas. There are community colleges in urban areas where nearly all entering freshmen are in need of at least one developmental course — and many of them are deficient in all of the basic skills. It may be that the greatest challenge in the years ahead for America's community colleges will be serving the unprepared, high-risk students.

Nearly all community colleges take on the task of developmental studies with great reluctance. Although the missions of these institutions usually include a reference to developmental studies, they are hardly ever offered with the vigor and enthusiasm of sophomore-level or professional courses. Most faculty do not want to teach developmental studies. They would rather teach their specialty of Shakespeare or calculus.

One can argue endlessly whether developmental studies or ESL or GED Prep are higher education. They are not. They are preparation for higher education. But why argue? Few others can or will take on the responsibility. And who wants to see the nation continue to decline simply because we argue whether it is higher education or not? Community colleges would do better as a movement to accept the reality that developmental studies are essential to the community they serve, and that developmental studies can work — indeed must work. Rather than accept the facts of illiteracy and the implications of such decay and failure, however, most community colleges limit their efforts in developmental studies. This is not totally the fault of the institutions. There is little support in the halls of the legislatures or even among the public for fighting illiteracy. Few understand how serious this problem has become; how difficult it is to overcome, and how dangerous it would be to fail. It would be opportune, therefore, for many community college faculties to take a new look now at their developmental studies programs to determine if they can meet better the challenge of illiteracy. Rather than view developmental studies as an afterthought, the future may well demand that literacy become the paramount objective; that more resources and more talent be devoted to literacy and developmental studies, and that students be held to higher achievement levels before entering credit courses.

So over the next 20 years, it may be that the number one task of the community college will be efforts to overcome illiteracy. As the result of an American school system that is a failure for many students, America's community colleges over the next several decades or longer will be forced to place a higher emphasis on developmental and literacy studies. Governing board members, chief executive officers, chief academic officers and faculties would do well to accept this reality and develop effective — indeed highly effective — programs of developmental studies, college preparatory studies, and ESL. The nation needs this initiative to remain strong and vital; the institutions need this initiative to have students, but mostly the students need this initiative as perhaps their only hope for success in the workplace. Although these are not popular tasks with most faculties, they must embrace them enthusiastically in the future if they are to carry out their central missions as comprehensive, community-centered institutions.

To accomplish the goal of a more broadly educated society, many more high school graduates must be attracted to — as well as be prepared for — college. This will require a greatly enhanced role for community colleges to help the elementary and secondary schools to prepare their students for college and to encourage them to take advantage of these higher educational opportunities. A changing America needs a system of education from kindergarten to post-graduate work that can, as "An American Imperative: Higher Expectations for Higher Education" prepared by the Wingspread Group on Higher Education recommended:

> In this new environment many more educators must be prepared to say: 'All of us, from pre-school to post-graduate, are in this together. It is not enough to complain about each other's failings. It is time to stop addressing the problem piecemeal. We must begin to work collaboratively on the system as a whole. It is no longer tolerable for so many in higher education to complain about the quality of those they admit, but do nothing to set higher standards and work with colleagues in K-12 schools to help students attain those standards. Our education system is in crisis; business-as-usual is a formula for national disaster.'

Few can any longer challenge the indictment that our schools do not work for many students. Indeed, many well-prepared students are sent to our colleges and universities each year. But far too many are ill-prepared — even unprepared — for the college experience. Community colleges (indeed, all of higher education) need to encourage the secondary schools to concentrate on the basic skills and on the basic knowledge required to produce broadly educated students prepared for the college experience. Furthermore, community colleges should vigorously provide pre-college programs and activities that complement and enrich those of the elementary and secondary schools. They should include college awareness efforts to encourage more young people to think about going to college, efforts about what preparation is needed for college and to inform them of the vast amounts of financial aid available to enable them to go to college.

Many pre-college activities have shown promise. The national Minorities in Engineering Project, for example, has proven that more students can be attracted to careers in engineering and science. These projects include complementary instruction in mathematics, science and the language arts, experiences with role models who are engineers, and taking advanced mathematics and science courses in high school. Many more similar programs are needed, so more students take a real college preparatory program.

Pre-college activities should include programs for young people and in-service programs for teachers. Successful programs have included instruction to high school students and teachers in computer technology; science and mathematics courses offered by the college at local high schools; mini-courses for high school students and research apprenticeships for minority students and many more. Community colleges have vast resources to bring to pre-college endeavors. What is lacking is adequate funding.

Both local school systems and community colleges should consider allocating relatively small portions of their budgets for these activities, which could pay off handsomely in higher secondary school graduation rates, more motivated students and fewer students in developmental courses at the community college. Community college faculty and staff need to see pre-college activities as a major way to help reduce the number of their students requiring developmental studies.

Community colleges also should increase their efforts to articulate their programs with the four-year colleges and universities and with the secondary schools. There will be a need for more programs of dual admissions and articulation between community colleges and four-year institutions. Students must know in advance what they have to do to transfer successfully with advanced standing and with all credits accepted. And high school students need to know what they have to do to be accepted into the college and into the program of their choice.

While placing a much greater emphasis on developmental and literacy studies, community colleges will need to expand and enrich their liberal arts programs and their general education offerings. Community college leaders and faculty need to see the relationship between larger and better programs of developmental and literacy studies and preparing more students broadly educated for a new world that rewards the highly educated with high-paying jobs and a high quality life.

C. A More Competent, More Adaptable Workforce

America today is part of a global economy — a global economy that traces its modern beginnings to the financial and economic systems created after World War II. These systems were designed to provide stability — which they have — and to create global markets operating as one. They also have led to the modern multi-national corporations, which to some degree are operating unregulated and uncontrolled by nation states and eroding the power of these states. Today within the global economy is a workforce that totals about 1.7 billion estimated to grow to about 3.1 billion by 2025, meaning the world's economy needs to create about 40 million jobs per year from now to 2025.

As a result of the globalization of the economy, America today has a knowledge-based economy that requires highly skilled workers — of which there is a shortage — and requires few unskilled workers — of which there are many competing for a limited number of jobs. For example, the nation has seen the loss of high-paying blue collar jobs such as the automobile workers, as United States' auto firms lost out to foreign competition or plants moved overseas. At the same time, America created millions of new jobs with the vast majority being low-paying, requiring few skills and leading to few opportunities in the service industries such as fast-food stores, gas stations, hotels and supermarkets. A key factor to consider in workforce development is that the relatively unskilled American worker must now compete with millions of people throughout the world willing to work for a fraction of their wage as a result of global economic integration. Furthermore, America's non-college educated workers have fewer skills than their counterparts in Germany, Japan and other industrial countries. (Interestingly, America's college-educated compare favorably with those in the other industrial countries.)

As the result of a global economy, there are jobs needed internationally — jobs such as biotechnologists, lawyers, economists and software developers. They make up about one-fifth of the nation's workforce. Meanwhile, technological advances such as robots and automated teller machines are reducing the demand for low-skilled workers for assembly lines, bank tellering and other jobs and helping to keep down their wages. There is a growing demand at the same time for highly educated workers.

Workers with college degrees now earn 57 percent more than high school graduates, according to the Economic Policy Institute, a research group based in Washington, D.C. The Institute reported that the average hourly wage for high school graduates fell 12 percent from 1979 to 1991, after factoring in inflation; remained flat for workers with college degrees and rose by eight percent for Americans with at least two years of graduate school.

Education has many benefits for the individual, as all of us in education understand. But it has a greater value for the society, as education is an investment in the future. This value was documented in a recent study conducted by the Census Bureau for the federal Department of Education. Based on interviews with managers and owners of about 3,000 businesses, it found that "a 10 percent increase in the educational attainment of a company's workforce resulted in an 8.6 percent increase in productivity." The survey found that a 10 percent increase in the value of such capital items as machinery, tools and building produced only a 3.4 percent increase in productivity.

What, then, will the American workforce of the future look like? What new jobs will there be? Few people are willing to venture a guess at this time, but the Department of Labor's Commission on Achieving Necessary Skills has produced a list of critical skills it thinks workers will need in the future: written and oral communication, critical analysis, interpersonal competence, the ability to obtain and use data, the capacity to make informed judgments, and the skills required in community life. We will need more highly educated men and women who can think critically, draw implications and make rational decisions. More and more they will need a greater knowledge of today's technology. Teaching students how to learn will be a critical component of tomorrow's community college curriculum, because workers are likely to operate in three or four different jobs in their employment lifetimes.

Many community colleges are already deeply involved in job training and retraining and in literacy and basic skills instruction to upgrade and retrain the workforce. A survey in 1990 showed that 71 percent of the 1,126 community colleges, junior colleges and technical institutes who were members of the American Association of Community Colleges operated federally-funded programs through their local Private Industry Councils, while 149 institutions conducted employment training and literacy programs sponsored and paid for directly by the private sector. Four federal programs provide millions of dollars each year for employment, training, welfare-to-work and related educational programs: the Jobs Training Partnership Act of

1982; the Family Support Act of 1988; the Job Opportunities and Basic Skills (JOBS) program, and the Carl D. Perkins Vocational and Applied Technology Education Act. As the list indicates, these efforts are fragmented and often have conflicting purposes, different program definitions and different delivery structures. Despite this extensive involvement in workforce development efforts, community colleges are not well represented on bodies formulating workforce development policies. As a result, community colleges are not used as extensively nor as effectively as they might be even though they have the capacity to deliver comprehensive training and educational services.

Because of the globalization of the economy, there will be an ever greater need in the future to upgrade and retrain the workforce. Community colleges would do well to seize this opportunity to help solve one of America's fundamental problems. It is likely that political and social forces will require nearly all of them to take on the gigantic task of upgrading and retraining America's workforce, because they have the capability and the flexibility to do it. It may be that no other agency — including community-based organizations — has the capability.

The community colleges' role in the upgrading and the retraining of the workforce will include its Associate Degree programs, its continuing education offerings, its career programs of all kinds, and its customized training efforts as well as others that have not yet been discovered. The needs will range from basic skills courses to advanced technological disciplines. And they will vary greatly from area to area.

In many instances, the community college will need to work with federal and state agencies to implement job training programs. Although these agencies in the past have turned to community-based organizations to provide these services, they are more and more using the community college — often because community colleges are less expensive and often produce better results. Community colleges also are more stable and more accountable and often can obtain other funds — including state aid — to help pay for these programs.

Community colleges do and should continue to work with welfare reform efforts that emphasize education and training to break the cycle of poverty. Too often, however, the expectations of the policymakers and bureaucrats administering these programs are unrealistic about how quickly and how successfully people can be educated and trained for employment. They want to do in six months what has not happened for some students during their entire elementary and secondary school careers. They want to overcome overnight negative attitudes about education and its values — attitudes and values that have developed over many years and that have been traditional within their communities.

As community colleges get more and more involved in workforce development efforts, they should always insist on realistic goals and objectives for programs and for students. All job training programs must lead to real employment opportunities. They should turn down grants and contracts that require them to produce what they realistically cannot do. Community colleges must retain integrity in the system — even if it means rejecting grants and contracts.

Community colleges should learn to work with local Private Industry Councils in particular, because they are mandated by federal law to determine what kinds of job training are needed and to select which agencies will provide them. Many community colleges are deeply involved in this process and are the major providers of job training under the Jobs Training Partnership Act. Most community colleges would be wise to be tuned-in to their local Private Industry Council — or whatever agency exists in the years ahead — because upgrading and retraining the workforce will be a top priority of America's tomorrow.

D. More Involved and Better Informed Citizenry

"We the People" reads our Constitution. This is the essence of our democratic form of government — a system that requires the participation — active participation — of all citizens. But it requires more than participation. It requires participation by an informed citizenry. Certainly, we do not have participation by a majority of our citizens today. Many are not well informed, and there are indications that today's voters are very susceptible to special interests, emotional appeals and issue-oriented columnists and broadcasters.

In many ways, our democratic system is not working well. Far too few adults are registered to vote; far too many who are registered to vote fail to go to the polls, and far too many citizens fail to participate in political or public affairs in any way. Many surveys indicate a lack of interest on the part of our citizens in the workings of our political system and in today's public issues at the local, state or national levels, and a lack of understanding of what our system of government is all about and the role each citizen must play. There is an obvious connection between the lack of civics teaching and the decline in what Thomas Jefferson called an "enlightened people." Why is this so? Again we can look to the failures of our educational system and to our TV broadcasters (augmented by Hollywood) who seek to entertain rather than inform.

One would expect that local school systems operating in a democratic society would give great emphasis to informing students about this system of government and the responsibilities and rights of each individual and to motivating them to participate. Such does not seem to be the case. A few young people are very active in public affairs and well-informed, but for the vast majority there is limited interest and limited knowledge. Again, one would expect that our television stations operating in a democratic society and licensed to operate by that society would place great emphasis on public affairs. There are some outstanding public affairs programs and extensive news coverage, but for the most part television stations are primarily interested in making money and have forgotten essentially their public trust. Furthermore, TV has attracted young people to its medium hour after hour, but hardly ever for public affairs offerings that would educate them to be responsible citizens for the future.

Television has been deadly for political discourse in another way: the vehicle for mean-spirited, negative advertising, which further frays the civic culture.

"It's certainly accurate to say that the quality of discourse has declined, and over time that's harmful because it erodes confidence in institutions and makes less clear the mandate of those elected," former Rep. Vin Weber, a Republican who is associated with Empower America, a conservative organization, said.

"I'm concerned that we've now devised a means of campaigning that creates an angry electorate which then vents its anger by voting no, no, no, no," Kathleen Hall Jamieson, dean of the Annenberg School at the University of Pennsylvania, said.

"If you go in and just vote no, you're not really licensing someone to govern."

Edward M. Fouhy, executive director of the Pew Center for Civic Journalism, called for some kind of citizen involvement in the electoral process "so that it's not just an insider game — an exercise where politicians raise large sums of money, consultants relieve them of that money, making commercials that are mostly negative, and it's all then covered by the Teddy White model of political journalism: Who's up, who's down, what's the nature of the ads."

There may be some hope in a developing movement called "civic journalism" whereby news organizations rethink the way they cover political campaigns. They would try to engage citizens by re-injecting their concerns into the debate through extensive interviewing, polls and public forums, for example.

Today, America is run by a minority, by voters who consider themselves independents rather than members of a political party, and by many voters who are more issue-oriented — often a single issue — than interested in the general welfare of the entire society.

As the most democratic of America's higher education institutions and as the people's college, the community college has a special role to play in attracting and motivating adults to a role of active and informed participants in a democratic society. But being a good citizen of the United States is no longer enough in a world in disarray and in a global economy. Today good citizenship also includes being attuned to foreign affairs politically, economically, diplomatically and culturally. America's "new" community college should broaden its mission to educate its constituents to their role as active and informed citizens.

Community colleges might set such goals as:

- Registering a vast majority of their constituents to vote;
- Encouraging a vast majority of registered voters to go to the polls for every election;
- Getting many more citizens involved in governmental, political, public and foreign affairs activities, and
- Offering many more public affairs forums and other public affairs programming to better educate their constituents about public issues, about their political system, about their governmental operations and about foreign affairs.

Community colleges have many resources to bring to an effort to educate the general public to a level of enlightened and informed voters. Most community colleges have Media Centers that could produce public affairs television and radio shows of all kinds – shows that could be both interesting and local. They could sponsor public affairs forums and workshops for their students, their faculties and staffs and for the general public. They could encourage student activities in current events, public issues and foreign affairs and they could encourage student governments to operate as a learning process with parties, campaigns, elections and polling. Many community colleges have faculty who could play a leading role in educating the public about the political process, public issues and foreign affairs.

They could be given release time to take on these tasks more actively and in a non-partisan fashion. The community college campus should become the local forum and center for public debate on the great public issues of the day — international, national and local. And community colleges could enroll more of their students in political science, government and current events courses and in local, state and national history courses that define the political process.

The Center for Civic Education, a nonprofit group, has proposed national educational standards for civics and government — voluntary standards for what children should know in academic subjects by the time they leave fourth, eighth and 12th grades.

"The strength and vitality of American democracy depend on insuring that our young people develop the knowledge, skills and dispositions necessary to become informed and responsible participants in our system of self-government," Charles N. Quigley, executive director of the Center for Civic Education, said.

But civics education does not end at the 12th grade — it is a lifelong process that should be engaged in by the community college movement. And the community colleges could fill the gap where adults did not get adequate civics education in the past. Perhaps the national standards for civics and government could be developed into a curriculum for adults and made available by all community colleges — a way to produce the "enlightened people" Thomas Jefferson yearned for and who are so desperately needed today.

A small percentage of each community college's operating budget should be allocated to educating the general public to be good citizens of the world, the nation, the state and locally. This is a small price to pay to preserve a system of government that provides "liberty and justice for all," provides us security from external and internal forces, and provides us with educations and a multitude of health, welfare, public safety and other services.

It is dangerous for a democracy to be controlled by a small minority and by those promoting special interests. If we, the people, do not take over our government, we will lose it. Once again it is the community college that should play a leadership role in providing citizen education, since our school systems and our media have failed to do so effectively.

E. A Broader, More Comprehensive System of Lifelong Learning

Lifelong learning has been a slogan for higher education for many years — a dream more than a reality. Even comprehensive community colleges talk a better game about lifelong learning than they play. The lifelong learning priority is almost always much lower than offerings that lead to a credential — any credential — and the resources allocated are usually starkly small.

In tomorrow's America, lifelong learning should and will play a greatly expanded role, so society can keep up with the knowledge explosion and with the fast-changing political, economic and social changes that will impact directly upon their lifestyle and quality of life. Again, it is the community college that is well-placed to provide these services extensively, inexpensively, and continuously. Lifelong learning departments in tomorrow's community college will serve youngsters as young as six or seven years old — perhaps even younger where they operate day care centers with an educational focus — to senior citizens.

Serving senior citizens is a new market for the community college. They represent an untapped market for many community colleges — a market rich in students and often rich in wealth. Why should senior citizens go to college or return to college? There are many reasons: to prepare for employment if necessary or desirable; for intellectual stimulation; for social interaction; for personal enrichment, or simply to learn for the sake of learning. Learning is not only enriching for senior citizens, but, as we learned at Union County College through the LIFE

(Learning Is For Ever) Center, it is also life-extending for some of them. And what a market! The number of senior citizens in America in the next 35 years will double to a total of 65 million people 65 years or over by 2025 — one in five of the population total. And the elderly population is getting older, making the need for intellectual stimulation even greater. And many will be prosperous with large pensions and many other financial assets. And many of them will be highly educated and ready for stimulating instruction. Many senior citizens will simply enroll in existing credit and continuing education offerings. But others may need courses customized to meet their individual needs. Still others will need to have the courses brought to them at their retirement homes, senior citizen housing projects, community centers and places of worship. As senior citizens live longer, they represent an emerging population needing many educational services. They will challenge the creativity and the imagination of community college leaders.

Some might argue that educating young people is the sole responsibility of the elementary and secondary schools. To a great degree that is true. But public schools in America are not performing well — particularly those in the cities. This is not to suggest that the community colleges take over and run the public schools. That is not their mission. But services to complement those of the public schools, to help prepare some young people better for the college experience, and to provide summer instruction for certain students are indeed appropriate — even necessary. Although the concept of pre-college activities is relatively new, there have been efforts in this area for many years. As early as the mid-'50s, Union County College (then known as Union College) offered a Science Seminar for Academically Talented High School Students. Its goal was to attract gifted high school students to careers in the sciences. And it worked.

As the problems of our public schools become more and more severe, the community college will be called upon to help solve these problems. The possibilities range from after-school programs for children whose parents are working to summer camps for gifted and talented youngsters, using existing facilities and resources productively. Some community colleges already assist in keeping school teachers current in their disciplines and in instructional methods. Community colleges could play an enormous role in assisting the local schools to continuously improve — and perhaps produce a better product. One could argue that it would be more economical to prepare students for college in their early days rather than spending millions on developmental and remedial education at the collegiate level. Furthermore, pre-college activities could attract more students to go to college — something the nation will require in the future to meet its new workforce needs. Some community colleges have learned, too, that pre-college activities are a very good student recruitment vehicle. The recently-enacted Two-Plus-Two Tech Prep initiative funded by the Carl Perkins Vocational and Applied Technology Education Act provides a vehicle for articulation of high school and community college programs. Easing the transition from high school to college and providing advanced standing in some instances are goals worth pursuing.

A special focus of lifelong learning in the future will be health education offerings, because Americans have a fascination about their health, spending more on health services than any other society in the world. Americans, according to the federal Commerce Department, now spend $1 trillion a year on health services. That's correct — $1 trillion — and it accounts for more than 15 percent of the nation's total output of goods and services. And it continues to grow. The Commerce Department forecasts it will continue to grow robustly even if the health care system is overhauled.

Americans want to keep up with the latest developments in medicine and many want to participate in physical activities to keep healthy. This fascination is likely to continue and probably will become more intense, as wellness is on the minds of many Americans. Community colleges are finding that they, too, have a role to play in educating the public to the advances in medical science. It is interesting to note how many federal agencies, health and social agencies and others are vying to be the leader in educating the public to the need for exercise, about nutrition, and how to fight high cholesterol, high blood pressure and obesity, for example. Such agencies as the National Centers for Disease Control and Prevention, the National Heart, Lung and Blood Institute and the President's Council on Physical Fitness and Sports would do well to enlist the 1,500-community college network to assist them with these efforts: a ready-made, nationwide network with experience and knowledge in reaching and educating the public.

Health education is often the responsibility of local hospitals and clinics, but community colleges, especially those with health professions and nursing programs and those affiliated with hospitals and medical schools, also can — and should — play a role in health education. Indeed, all community colleges can be involved in health education as well as constructive fitness and recreational activities and personal enrichment offerings. Wellness activities can take the form of classes, workshops and seminars, but they can also include fitness, aerobics and similar activities. As the average age of student bodies continues to rise, these kinds of activities become more and more appropriate for students. But they can also be used to attract new audiences to the community colleges — busy adults, even senior citizens — who need supervised physical activities.

A continuing education opportunity for many community colleges will be programs of professional continuing education for nurses and allied health personnel. With the major advances in health care, it is crucial that all health care personnel be kept current in their fields. Some states mandate continuing education for health care personnel and others are likely to follow suit. Some community colleges discovered how creative and effective they could be in professional continuing education for nurses by devising programs to attract them back into the profession during the last nursing shortage in the '80s. Similar programs can be developed for the allied health professions as the need arises. These shortages seem to come in cycles, and community college leaders should be alert to them and provide appropriate programs.

Continuing education for all professionals will be an emerging need, as the knowledge explosion continues and as society changes. Professionals in all fields will find it ever more difficult to keep current in their fields. The community college already has in place the mechanisms to help professionals meet their continuing education needs. Working with professional organizations to help assess these needs, to help develop programs and to provide instructors are ways that community colleges can meet this need effectively and efficiently and with integrity.

Lifelong learning will make extensive use of the communications superhighway now in its early development. Telecourses will be one vehicle and teleconferences and self-directed learning will be others. The opportunities to bring information and instruction to the general public is almost unlimited — off-campus and in the home. Learning how to do it effectively and inexpensively and in a timely fashion will be the challenge. Community colleges are in the forefront of these efforts and are likely to be the major player in so-called distance learning in the future.

Lifelong learning can and should encompass every facet of life, providing whatever educational services society needs. Only a lack of creativity and imagination as well as resolve will prevent the community college from being the national leader in lifelong learning, as the movement has the flexibility to do it all. But only if it accepts the challenge and seizes the opportunity. With such leadership, the face of America's educational system could be changed dramatically — dramatically for the better. Community colleges in the years ahead should consider every adult a potential consumer of its lifelong learning offerings, and they should organize offerings to meet their needs whether it be for basic skills or ESL instruction or sophisticated technological instruction in computers, robotics, or some other field we have yet to find or invent. Enrollments in lifelong learning offerings in the future are likely to far exceed those in degree programs and the range of disciplines offered are likely to be much wider and much more diverse. Lifelong learning will be the cutting edge of the community college movement and community colleges will lead the way — providing they seize the opportunity quickly and dynamically.

Why should America look to its community colleges to produce a more broadly educated society, a more competent, more adaptable workforce, a more involved and better informed citizenry and a broader, more comprehensive system of lifelong learning to serve a changing America within a changing world? Because they are accessible, open to all segments of society, and economical. They also have close ties to elementary and secondary schools and to colleges and universities, they have faculty and staff attuned to these missions and they have the administrative structures and expertise to implement them.

Part VII

Achieving Tomorrow's Community College

As America continues to change within a dramatically changing world, every community college must determine its own destiny to serve its local constituency and to be part of a national network of community colleges. There are no magic wands to solve problems and to meet the challenges facing today's community colleges. Each institution will need to look at itself honestly and thoroughly to determine where it is and where it wants to go.

But there are some key areas every community college should consider as it prepares for the 21st century and beyond. These areas include a dedication to help to develop:

A more broadly educated society;

A more competent and more adaptable workforce;

A more involved and better-informed citizenry, and

A broader, more comprehensive system of lifelong learning.

Tomorrow's community college will require a dedication to allocating its resources primarily to teaching and learning. This means hiring more and better faculty, tutors, mentors and librarians — all those who directly impact upon learning. This means faculty salaries should far exceed those of the athletic coaches. This means there will be adequate resources for the equipment, books and materials needed in the teaching/learning process; there will be great flexibility in meeting the different learning styles and the different educational achievement levels of students, and there will be faculty who are prepared to provide multiple modes of instruction better to meet the needs of students. This means class sizes will be appropriate to the courses being taught and to the students enrolled in them.

Tomorrow's community college will require a dedication to program review and evaluation, to revising programs as community needs change, and to developing new programs to serve better the needs of their constituents. This embraces all programs: credit or without credit, remedial or developmental and on-campus or off-campus.

Tomorrow's community colleges will require a dedication to select chief executive officers who are first and foremost leaders — both educational leaders and community leaders. They should provide the drive and the initiative to prepare their institutions to face a changing America within a changing world; to face a global economy requiring highly skilled, highly educated men and women; to face a declining political system in need of renewal and in need of involved and informed citizens, and to face the reality of an educational system that is failing to meet the needs of today's complex society. Presidential searches should be broader, more extensive and deeper, and chief executive officers should be selected with the greatest of care to insure that only the very best are hired. And the first and foremost criterion must be the ability to lead.

Tomorrow's community colleges will require a dedication to planning — particularly strategic planning. Institutions should understand what they are and where they want to go. These decisions should be made on the basis of good research, hard data and on rational judgment. And they should honestly and comprehensively evaluate and assess what they are doing and determine if they are truly meeting their goals and objectives — particularly evaluating how well they are serving the needs of their students and the needs of the area they serve.

Tomorrow's community colleges will require a dedication to cooperation and collaboration with business and industry, with the professions, with the elementary and secondary schools, with federal, state, county and local governments and agencies, with health, social and welfare agencies, with community-based organizations, with public safety agencies, and with other colleges and universities and other educational institutions. This cooperation and collaboration will be dedicated to offering higher quality programs, courses and other educational activities and to operating more effectively and more efficiently — truly doing more with less.

Tomorrow's community college must be dedicated to affordability — for students and for taxpayers. It must be a major goal to make its services available to a broader segment of the population by providing low tuition and by operating as efficient and effective institutions. Since community colleges are affordable — inexpensive to the student and to the taxpayer — they will be especially important in the future as higher education is placing itself "beyond the financial reach of many middle-class families," according to former New Jersey Governor Tom Kean, president of Drew University, Madison, N.J. Kean added that without restructuring "higher education will once again become the province of the wealthy, denied to the majority of Americans."

"Nobody should be denied the opportunity to succeed simply because they were born of the wrong parents or without wealth," Kean said. He was not talking about the community college specifically, but more than any other type of institution the community college already carries out Kean's goal — opportunity for all to succeed in higher education.

Surely, the newly formed Commission on the National Investment in Higher Education, headed by Kean and the chief executive officer of McGraw-Hill, Joseph Dionne, should look at the community college as part of its goal "to provide a dynamic national discussion of the future financial foundation of higher education and its capacity to meet public needs."

"In a society in which knowledge is increasingly our principal form of capital, we cannot afford to limit access to education," Kean said. "There is no overall, well-planned policy now. Nobody decided that we are going to deny opportunity, but that is what's happening."

Community colleges must not let this happen. They must remain affordable by providing the opportunity of higher education to all segments of society.

Tomorrow's community colleges will require a dedication to resource development in the broadest sense involving both the private and public sectors — all levels of the public sector. This means the federal government must fund adequately a student financial aid program that truly makes available the opportunities of higher education to economically disadvantaged and middle class students. And it means that the federal government must play a larger role in supporting community colleges to carry out national goals such as job training, welfare reform, literacy, drug and alcohol abuse education, broadly educate men and women, and more informed and involved voters operating in a renewed political system. (Participating community colleges could be known as National Goals Institutions such as the Land Grant Institutions of a previous era.) The states, too, should be encouraged to develop a system of State Goals Institutions and fund their particular initiatives. And the entire private sector should be encouraged to support generously the community college movement as it takes on new missions with new responsibilities.

Tomorrow's community college will require a dedication to the use of technology for learning and teaching. As community colleges attempt to implement a broader mission, they will need to give serious and careful attention to the impact of technology upon the learning and teaching environments on their campuses. Clearly, computers and TV will play a role, but how significant will they be? It is probably too early to tell. We know TV can have a profound impact upon learning, but only a positive impact with responsible programming. And that seems to be true for computers as well. It seems that the hardware far outdistances the software to support it — particularly for educational purposes.

Because of the emergence of technology, learning by doing may replace the all-knowing teacher who lectures to a captive audience who must learn at a mutual pace, receive information selected by the teacher and have little control over what and how fast they will learn. This kind of instruction could be replaced by a teacher who already has taught students how to use a computer, who will serve as a facilitator as students teach themselves by accessing the information highway via their computers and by the use of interactive video programs. For example, they could learn mathematics, science and literature at the same time at their own pace. And fast learners could help slower learners. This is not a dream, according to Seymour Papert, an MIT professor and a visionary for high-tech classrooms.

"This is not just imaginary science fiction. It is close at hand," Papert, who developed the Logo computer language, said. "It's irresponsible for us not to take (technology) seriously."

Some theorists see the marriage of the computer and the telephone as a communications revolution that could in the future exceed the scope and scale of the printing press. According to Paul L. Staffo, a director of the Institute for the Future, Menlo Park, California, "The growth and innovation has come from machines talking to machines on people's behalf." He cited Coke machines that carry numbers to dial distribution centers for refills when supplies are dwindling.

Multimedia and an information infrastructure with interactive capability today can link schools, libraries and other agencies. They hold great promise for education, providing students with the ability to share ideas and to communicate with each other.

"The information superhighway is real, and it is coming to a television/telephone computer near you," Paul C. O'Brien, chairman of NYNEX New England, predicted. "It will have as profound an impact on the way we live, learn and earn as did the infrastructure that supported the Industrial Age. It will support current and new industries that rely heavily on information. That includes just about every facet of modern life. The danger for our society — as a political democracy — is the possible creation of information 'haves' and 'have nots.'"

Without question technology is having a major impact upon society — more than most people realize. But society has great difficulty evaluating the impact of technology. At first blush, society overacts, then loses faith and eventually finds that technology has a greater impact upon them than ever imagined. This truism must be kept in mind as community colleges consider the use of technology for learning and teaching.

But, most of all, tomorrow's community college — indeed any college — must be an institution of higher education. (This may seem obvious, but not all community colleges and not all four-year colleges are really institutions of higher education. They are sometimes something less.) An institution of higher education must serve adults and they must recruit students who are there voluntarily and enroll because they want to be there and because they can benefit from the services offered. They must offer instruction that is intellectually stimulating and delves into each discipline in considerable depth, and they must aim to produce broadly educated men and women who can live and work in a modern, civilized world and a democratic society.

And tomorrow's community college will need programs or activities that are distinctive and unique. They give the institution a place in the sun and enhance its image — not insignificant factors in the development and growth of an institution. Certainly, football put Notre Dame on the map even though it lays proper claim to outstanding academic programs. A Nobel Laureate will, of course, bring distinction to any institution. Such unique or distinctive programs or activities, however, must be part of the institution's basic mission, and must not detract in any way from the institution's operations. It may be that state coordinating boards and accreditating agencies may not call for distinctiveness or uniqueness in their definition of quality, but all institutions have — and need — such programs or activities.

All of this is a great deal to ask of the community college movement that is still not fully accepted nor fully understood by the general public, community leaders and particularly four-year colleges and universities. To make it happen, the nation must produce leaders who will be the CEOs of these new community colleges — leaders who are strong and savvy, leaders with high ethical standards and leaders who have a vision to make tomorrow's community college a reality. In addition, the nation must produce faculty members who want to teach and mentor — faculty dedicated to tomorrow's community college. The task of producing tomorrow's community college leaders and faculty will fall primarily to our major universities. Unfortunately, the universities hardly realize that a giant called the community college has arisen. They have failed to recognize the size and scope of the community college movement and they have failed to recognize the important role they could and should play in developing community college leaders and faculty.

Therefore, tomorrow's community college must adopt and implement a broader, richer, more diverse mission that includes a dedication to developing a more broadly educated society, a more competent and more adaptable workforce, a more involved and better-informed citizenry, and a broader, more comprehensive system of lifelong learning. This broader, richer, more diverse mission for the community college movement that includes a leadership role to help in a significant way to solve some of America's major problems will require the establishment of a nationwide network of community colleges — a network of institutions we might call National Goals Institutions. Just imagine the force, the impact of a coordinated system of 1,200 to 1,500 community colleges geared to similar objectives with adequate funding to carry them out. Indeed, such a system could take on a vital issue such as illiteracy and deal with it effectively — in a way that would have real impact. And it would have a national impact. Furthermore, it would be a system that would develop partnerships and collaborations with many other agencies to help carry out a national goal such as retraining the workforce in America. Such a system, furthermore, would facilitate cooperation in the development of curriculum and alternative modes of instruction including the use of the "new" technology as well as faculty and staff development techniques and activities. But it would be a system operated locally and geared to the specific needs of that locality. Programs would be geared to those constituents and their needs.

Community colleges bring to this system institutions in every part of the nation, including those in every Congressional District and in every state, and those in urban, suburban and rural environs. It would be a system with extensive facilities and experienced faculties and staffs. But most importantly it would be a system with vast experience in dealing with community services and with the unique needs of adults; with faculty and staff empathetic to the needs of adults, including the economically and educationally disadvantaged and minorities, and those with all educational achievement levels. Most of all community colleges bring to such a system the flexibility to serve all segments of society, as flexibility is the key to opportunity. Community colleges also bring to the system well-organized, highly experienced administrative units geared to providing community services. These units could rapidly and decisively grapple with an issue such as workforce development, because most of them are already deeply engaged in these efforts. But today's efforts to diminish illiteracy, for example, are meager in relationship to the size and scope of the problem. Imagine what a nationwide, coordinated effort with adequate funding could do!

Only the federal government has the resources to develop a system of National Goals Institutions utilizing America's 1,200 or so community colleges. It will only happen if the community colleges endorse it, support it and fight for it. This is a most difficult task in an environment in which the public is turning its back on government, because it does not trust government to solve its problems. But a system of National Goals Institutions is an idea for all Americans because it would serve all facets of society. And it would take on major issues America needs to solve — and solve quickly.

Can this broader, more comprehensive mission be provided by a community college system starving for adequate resources? Yes. But only if more funds are provided, particularly major assistance from the federal government — perhaps in the form of National Goals Institutions — and greatly increased funding from the states, other public agencies, and the private sector, and if our great universities face up to their responsibility to produce leaders and faculty for the community colleges. Tomorrow's community colleges will require and will deserve nothing less, because their constituents require and deserve nothing less and because a changing America within a changing world deserves nothing less.

Acknowledgements

A project of this scope could not have been accomplished without significant assistance from others. Those who read the entire manuscript and made valuable contributions include: Jean Benisch, Dr. Patricia Biddar. Frank H. Blatz, Jr., Barbara Bowley, Virginia Busch, Mary Jane Clem, Veronica Clinton, Camille Cormier, Dr. John R. Farrell, Jr., Dr. Kenneth W. Iversen, the late Elizabeth I. Kellogg, Linda S. Leifer, Sidney F. Lessner, Kathleen Longo, Dr. Kenneth C. MacKay, Dr. Albert E. Meder, Jr., Dr. Nan Parmentier, Frank J. Peterpaul, Victor M. Richel, David Riley, Dr. Robert Schipa and Jan Zymroz.

A special role was played by Ms. Clinton and Ms. Longo, who read and re-read draft-after-draft and made constructive suggestions for their improvement. After all their good efforts, any errors or omissions are totally mine.

Appreciation is expressed to Mr. Lessner and Mr. Richel for their continuing encouragement to move the project forward. Their confidence in the project is hereby gratefully acknowledged. I would be most remiss not to express my appreciation to Alberta (Bert) Matyas, who typed and re-typed (she actually used a computer) each draft and the many revisions with good cheer and continuous encouragement, deciphering my comments and changes accurately and with amazing speed.

I also must acknowledge the special role played by Dr. MacKay and Dr. Meder whose insights about the community college and higher education were instrumental in the completion of this essay.

And I must acknowledge the special research endeavors of Ms. Bowley and Dr. Biddar whose efforts were crucial. Hopefully I have not forgotten anyone who contributed to this project. If I did, I apologize to them.

DATE DUE

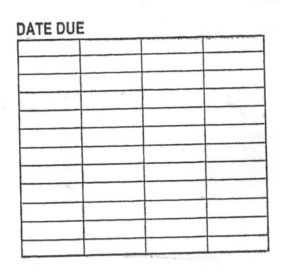

DEMCO